STRANGE PEOPLE

THE UnXPLAINED

STRANGE
PEOPLE

JAMIE STOKES

p

First published in 2000 by Parragon

Parragon
Queen Street House
4 Queen Street
Bath BA1 1HE, UK

Produced by Magpie Books, an imprint of
Constable Robinson Ltd, London

ISBN 0-75253-594-3

Illustrations courtesy of Fortean Picture Library and Popperfoto

Page design by Sandie Boccacci

A copy of the British Library Cataloguing-in-Publication Data
is available from the British Library

Printed and bound in the EC

For Agnieszka

Contents

Contents •

Introduction

● ●

Sometime in July of 1999 a very special child was born. Nobody knows exactly when or where. Nobody knows if this child was male or female, or even if it lived for any more than a few hours. Was this infant some kind of modern Messiah, or perhaps the result of a breakthrough in genetic science? Perhaps, but most likely this was an unremarkable creature, indistinguishable and unnoticed among one of the world's thriving human concentrations. Whatever its place or time of birth the child did have a unique quality that we can be certain of, a quality unprecedented in the history of our species. He or she was the six-billionth living human being.

Everyone thinks they know people pretty well. Almost all of us fleetingly meet thousands of people during the course of our lives and form relationships of one kind or another with hundreds. A cliché that rings true with everyone from the cosmopolitan traveller to the provincial homebody bears repeating: "everybody's different". Think about what that means today. It means that there are six billion distinct individuals on this planet. Each with totally unique features of character, physiology and mentality. If you met one new person every day you could hope to meet a little over 27,000 people in the course of a full lifetime –

that's less than 4,000th of one per cent of the world population – and none of them would be even remotely similar. The chances are that even among this tiny sample you would come across people whose experiences or characteristics would startle you. In the context of such a huge range of individuals the possibilities become mind-boggling.

In a world of six billion individuals, plus the few other billions who have lived during recorded history, there are some unique examples. These are individuals whose physical or mental characteristics have set them so far outside the range of our everyday experience that we literally have no idea what to make of them. They are clearly human (in most cases), they look like us and behave like us most of the time, but some appear to have powers or abilities that seem simply supernatural. Others report experiences so far outside the norms of our own lives that it is often tempting to dismiss these reports as the product of mental illness or deliberate fraud.

Simple physiological variation in people is a good way to illustrate how this happens. Carl Lewis, one of the fastest men on earth, can run a hundred metres in around 9.6 seconds. This doesn't sound startling until you consider what an incredibly unique physiology this ability represents. Ninety-nine per cent of the rest of the human race could not run one hundred metres in under ten seconds, no matter if they were trained from the day they were born. It's simply beyond their physical ability. Ninety-nine per cent of the remaining percentage may be able to break the ten-second barrier, but could not approach Lewis's athletic achievement.

In the context of six billion individuals those figures

make a Carl Lewis about as likely as winning a lottery jackpot every week for a year, and then being struck by lightning before you have a chance to spend the money. Of course Lewis is no more unique than you or I – the particular physical characteristics that each one of us possesses is just as statistically unlikely as his. The point is that, in Lewis's case, his uniqueness happens to have put him right at the edge of the possible range of human athletic ability. Almost all of the rest of us are bunched up right in the middle of that range. Even if you were pretty good at sports at school, compared to Carl Lewis you are effectively nowhere.

Most human characteristics are like this. If you study height, weight, brain size or a whole range of other measurable characteristics, you find an overwhelming majority of individuals clustered closely around an average figure, and a very few individuals scattered across a range of extreme possibilities. In the case of height, ninety-nine per cent of us are between about 1.3 metres and 1.9 metres. The shortest recorded human adult, Pauline Musters ("Princess Pauline"), stood only 59cm (23.2in), the tallest, Robert Pershing Wadlow, stood 272cm (8ft 11.1in).

As remarkable as these individuals were, they are not totally beyond belief. But what if somebody reported a human who was only ten centimetres tall, or one who was ten metres tall. Most people would agree that in the case of physical size we can tell that these figures are just absurd. While we are prepared to accept the possibility of a man nearly three metres tall we would simply dismiss a report of a man ten metres tall, and we would be right to do so. Similarly, who would give a second thought to a man said to weigh more than a blue whale, or a man who lived a normal life without a brain?

Unfortunately, the last case is medically recorded fact. So how can our instinct be wrong about this? In the case of height or weight, we do not easily make mistakes because these are things we understand implicitly. As physical beings we understand that a human ten metres tall is absurd not because we have never seen one anywhere near that height, but because we know it just wouldn't work. Such a creature would never be able to support its own weight let alone breathe or move.

Science backs up instinct in this case, the materials of the human body are simply not up to the job in terms of stresses and load-bearing properties. This is stuff our instincts are good at. We all know that jumping from high windows is unwise and very few people break their arms by trying to catch falling concrete blocks. However, in the case of people without brains our instincts let us down because the knowledge needed to make a realistic assessment of such cases doesn't come naturally to us.

Many of the fundamental precepts of modern science are completely contrary to our instinctive understanding of the world. Because everybody knows that the Earth is a sphere, that it revolves around the sun, and about our close relationship to chimpanzees, we tend to forget how contrary to our own instincts these truths are. If it turns out that a person can live a perfectly normal life without a brain we may be forced to accept that this is just another outrageous affront to our accepted view of the world. The question is, how many other truths just as outrageous are there waiting for us out there?

People do some incredible things and incredible things happen to some people. It seems clear that we simply cannot trust our instincts to tell us what is possible and what is impossible. Our understanding and expectations of the world work fine ninety-nine per cent of the time, but occasionally we just have to accept that the incredible is real. Unfortunately many of the cases of remarkable individuals and unbelievable occurrences happened long ago, or are no more than unsubstantiated stories. Without evidence we cannot rely on science to help us find the truth. As you discover the incredible stories within these pages just remember, truth can exist without proof.

Albertus Magnus

· ·

Magician or scientist?

One bleak winter's day in 1263, guests began arriving for a very special feast at a convent in Cologne. Among them was William II, Prince of Holland, but the assembled company were to be honoured not merely by the presence of royalty, but by the presence of the greatest genius and magician of their age – Albertus Magnus. Once assembled, the guests were perplexed to find a great table set in the gardens of the convent. Everything was decked with snow and bitterly cold. As their host emerged and bade them sit with him an incredible transformation took place. The snows disappeared as warm sunlight flooded the garden and sweet spring flowers bloomed all around. Summer birds flitted through the air and there on the table a sumptuous spread was revealed. The comments of the guests are not recorded – perhaps they expected nothing less from the man who was known throughout Europe as the Universal Doctor, worker of miracles.

In an age of darkness and ignorance a few men stood out for their almost supernatural learning, wisdom and saintliness (Magnus was himself canonized in 1932). Thomas Aquinas, Magnus's beloved pupil, Roger Bacon, Bartholomew of England, William of Auvergne, Vincent of Beauvais and the great poet Dante all illuminated these dark times. All of these men were profoundly religious and most held influential positions in the church (Magnus was Bishop of Ratisbon). In the thirteenth century the church dominated Europe politically and spiritually, and it was a very different institution to the closed and conservative Catholic church that has lost almost all power and influence in our age. Inquiries into all manner of occult and esoteric disciplines were carried out by these men, sometimes with the encouragement of their superiors. At that time there was no distinction between alchemy and chemistry, magic and psychology. Many scholars and churchmen openly sought the secrets of the transmutation of base metals into gold or of the formulation of the elixir of eternal life. Perhaps a few found them. The old fears that these studies were traps set by the devil were losing ground in an atmosphere of supreme confidence in the abilities of humankind. Much of modern science has its roots in the studies and methods of these remarkable individuals.

In his day Albertus Magnus was popularly regarded as a miracle worker, a holder of incredible secrets and a man of unmatched wisdom. Today, those who give credence to the incredible tales of the good doctor's powers fall into two camps. Some attribute his miracles to supernatural power gained from contact with a hidden spirit world that his magical studies gave him access to. Others point to his vast range of scientific works, and regard him as a great scientist who was able to amaze and perplex the superstitious using the advanced scientific knowledge he had acquired. Most agree, however, that he was a man of genius whose way of thinking was perhaps centuries ahead of its time.

Magnus was certainly an alchemist, his most celebrated text *On Alchemy* contains a wealth of information for the prospective miracle worker. Among its pages of minutely described experiments, observations and speculations is this set of strict rules to be observed by anyone embarking on this ancient and powerful study:

Directions to Alchemists

1. The alchemist must be silent and discreet. To no one should he reveal the fruits of his operations.

2. He shall live in loneliness, remote from men. His house should have two or three rooms devoted entirely to his work.

3. He shall choose the right hour for his operations.

4. He must be patient and persevering in character.

5. He will operate according to the rules: the trituration, the sublimation, the fixation, the calcination, the solution, the distillation and the coagulation.

6. He will use only glass vessels or glazed pottery.

7. He must be rich enough to afford the expense which these works demand.

8. And finally he will avoid contact with princes and rulers.

This curious mix of scientific and arcane advice is a clear example of the split in Magnus's philosophy. References to the processes of distillation and sublimation and the advice to use only glass or glazed pottery vessels, to prevent contamination of the materials, would make sense to a modern chemist. The reference to "the right hour for his operations" is less clear, but almost certainly refers to careful observation of astrological signs and portents to decide when conditions are right for success. The demands that the alchemist must be secretive and apart from the rest of mankind are characteristics that have marked out sages and magicians since Neolithic times. In keeping with his own advice Magnus never revealed if he had succeeded in transmuting metals into gold, but he was widely believed to have manufactured a stone that could perform this and other marvels. It was said that the power of this stone allowed him to turn winter into summer for the feast at Cologne.

Magnus also wrote about the magical properties of gems and rare stones in his work on minerals. He speaks of experiencing the powers of these stones personally – a claim he often used to validate the most mundane of his experiments and which has earned him a place among the fathers of modern science – but never describes exactly what preparations were needed to extract such magical properties.

Those who claim that Albertus Magnus was simply a scientist centuries ahead of his time point to the persistent story that he had an android as a personal servant. This incredible automata was said to have been built by Magnus using metals and precious stones prepared in his alchemy laboratories, and welded together in accordance with a strict sequence

The properties of gems and precious minerals

The amethyst: Acts against inebriation; creates alertness; ends quarrels; fosters the acquisition of knowledge and promotes intelligence.

The beryl: Overcomes laziness; soothes pain in the liver; stops hiccoughs; cures watery eyes; preserves peace in the home.

The emerald: Proves chastity when taken in an infusion; increases the owner's wealth; makes the owner persuasive and can cure epilepsy.

The agate: Strengthens the teeth and bones; drives away devils and melancholic spirits; cures stomach aches and drives away serpents.

The diacodos (a mineral unknown to modern science): Excites the activity of phantoms but loses its power when brought into contact with a corpse.

of astrological alignments that gave the machine magical powers. This robot servant – very similar to the devilish "familiars" reputedly used by witches and mages – was said to have the shape of a man and to have the power of speech and thought.

Could a thirteenth-century priest really have created an android in an era when even clockwork was in its infancy? What could have powered such a machine,

Albertus Magnus – magician or scientist?

what kind of materials would be needed and how could Magnus have had the detailed knowledge of human anatomy needed to create a robot that looked and behaved like a man? According to legend the talking robot annoyed Magnus's protégé Thomas Aquinas, so much that he smashed it to pieces one night with a hammer. Aquinas was said to have built a similar marvel many years later, using the knowledge he had inherited from his master. Interestingly this is not the only case of technology appearing hundreds of years out of place. Another thirteenth-century sage, a French rabbi named Jechiele, apparently had an electric lamp and played practical jokes on callers by shocking them with an electrified door knob. Among the many alchemists of the era most died in poverty or gave up their quests, although some seem to have acquired vast wealth. One such man was Nicolas Flamel, accredited scribe to the University of Paris. Born fifty years after the death of Magnus, Flamel is said to have discovered secret writings belonging to the great man and to have learned his secrets.

Could it be that Albertus Magnus and a small group of other men made discoveries far ahead of their time in that heady period of history? Did they share these secrets with a select band of students who they thought ready to deal with such profound revelations about the nature of the world – Thomas Aquinas among them? If so, what could have been the source of this knowledge, and what might they have known that we have forgotten?

The Miraculous, Deathless Count

•••••••••••••••••••••••••••••••••••

Who was the Count de Saint Germain?

In February of 1784 a man lay dying in the small town of Eckenforde, Schleswig-Holstein (now part of Germany). He suffered from rheumatism and bouts of depression and appeared to be in his mid-seventies. He was a slight man who had maintained his lifelong habit of sober dressing, politeness and impeccable manners. Not a remarkable picture, but not long after this quiet death in a quiet eighteenth-century German town, Charles, Prince of Hesse-Cassel, declared the deceased to be "one of the greatest sages who ever lived", and reports began to circulate that he would return from beyond the grave, or that he had never died at all. The Prussian king, Frederick the Great, called him "the man who could not die". Death was just another episode in the incredible life of the Count de Saint Germain – one of the most remarkable and mysterious figures of recent history.

The remarkable count first came to the attention of the world in the summer of 1756 when he appeared among the fashionable circles of Parisian society. Introducing himself as the Count de Saint Germain, the stranger caused an immediate stir not least by his habit of dressing in sinister black – a startling contrast to the gaudy male fashions of the day. His collection of fabulous diamond rings and the diamond-encrusted buckles that adorned his boots also attracted attention and seemed to indicate that he was a genuine aristocrat, although nobody in Paris could identify the dapper middle-aged man. Initial suspicions soon turned to delight as the mysterious count charmed French nobility with his manners, intelligence and incredible range of talents. He was an excellent pianist, violinist and singer, he could speak Spanish, Portuguese, Greek, Italian, Russian, Chinese, Arabic, Sanskrit, English, German and French fluently, but above all he was an enthralling conversationalist who seemed to possess an encyclopaedic knowledge of any subject that anyone cared to bring up.

Even more remarkable talents became apparent when the count cured a young woman at the court of mushroom poisoning. It emerged that the count had come to Paris in the company of the Marshal de Belle-Isle, and that he had miraculously cured the marshal of an illness he had contracted during a military campaign. Rumours of supernatural powers had already begun to circulate among the fashionable salons when the Countess von Gery, whose husband had been the French ambassador in Venice forty years before, asked to meet the count as she recalled meeting a man of the same name in the Italian city.

She found him excellent company and thought he seemed very familiar. Turning the conversation towards the subject of Venice, she asked if it was possible that she had met his father there many years before. The count smiled, shook his head and confessed that it was actually him that she had known.

The countess was confused by this since the man she had known in Venice all those years before, and who looked so like the count, had been in his mid-forties – apparently he hadn't aged a day. The countess expressed her doubts but Saint Germain was able to provide so many details of their acquaintance in Venice that she became convinced – and a little alarmed. "I am very old," remarked the count in reply to her questions, at which the countess exclaimed, "You must be a devil!" A remarkable change came over the man. He turned pale and began to tremble violently. "Please, no such names," he whispered and then left the room still trembling and doubled over with cramps. Gossip about the meeting raced through influential society – reaching even the royal family. People began to whisper about the ancient tale of the Wandering Jew, and many began to believe that the count could be this legendary figure.

The story of the Wandering Jew seems to have first come into Europe among the many fabulous tales brought back by knights returning from the crusades. It concerns a Jew who lived at the time of Christ – an underling in the palace of Pontius Pilate, the Roman governor who sentenced Jesus to death. This Jew, who some sources name Cartaphilus, was present at the trial and expressed no sympathy for the supposed Messiah. Later, as Jesus was goaded through the streets of Jerusalem on his way to the place of execution, Cartaphilus was among the crowds that lined the way. Jesus was dragging the cross on which he was to be crucified up the steep slopes of Calvary. He stopped momentarily to rest and Cartaphilus, eager to see the parade reach its gruesome conclusion, stepped out of the crowd and told him to hurry up.

Jesus rounded on the man and said calmly, "I shall go now, but thou shalt wait until my return," then he turned and resumed his final march, leaving Cartaphilus speechless with fear. Years passed and the terrible truth began to dawn on Cartaphilus. His friends and family aged and died, yet he had not grown a day older since that fateful hour on the road to Calvary. Cartaphilus knew his fate, he would wander the Earth until the day Christ returned. The doomed man packed up his belongings and tramped out of town into the mists of time.

Throughout the Middle Ages pilgrims and travellers told tales of a strange man they met on the road, who had incredible powers, seemed to be insane or possessed, and spoke of knowing Christ. In 1228 an Armenian bishop visiting St Albans astonished his hosts by claiming to have dined with a man who said he was Cartaphilus. But could the Count de Saint Germain possibly be the same man, and how could the cultured denizens of Paris believe that he was? This was the Age of Reason and Paris was the intellectual and cultural capital of Europe – Voltaire was at the height of his career, the world's first encyclopaedia was being compiled, and science was the new religion.

As the count's fame spread he attracted the interest of the king himself, who invited him to court. As always Saint Germain bewitched his hosts with his seemingly endless talents and knowledge. Apparently he performed many marvels that indicate a profound knowledge of science and even alchemy. Claiming to possess knowledge of a secret method of removing flaws from gemstones, the count took one of the king's diamonds worth 6000 francs and returned it later, now valued by a jeweller at 10,000 francs. In the presence of another remarkable eighteenth-century figure, the adventurer Casanova, the count is said to have transmuted silver into gold. While in Paris Saint Germain set up a factory that used a revolutionary new method of dyeing silks and softening leather, an enterprise that added substantially to his already large fortune. Could it be that this man held scientific knowledge far in advance of his time, or even of secrets that have since been forgotten?

If indeed he had been wandering the world for nearly two thousand years, who can say what strange and arcane arts the count may have learned down the centuries. Many of the scientific achievements of Egyptian, Chinese and Arabic civilizations have astonished modern researchers; could the count have known some of their secrets – using the knowledge to provide himself with a vast fortune down the ages, and perhaps even manipulating the course of history. Saint Germain's knowledge of history was certainly encyclopaedic. Scholars never tired of trying to catch him out on obscure points of ancient history, only to be astounded by the count's seeming first-hand knowledge of an event that had taken place many centuries before. It is said that he greatly alarmed one lady of the court by recounting family secrets to her that he had heard from an ancestor of hers on the battlefield of Marignano.

The count himself never confirmed or denied that he was indeed the Wandering Jew of legend. On several occasions witnesses heard him speak of events in the New Testament as if he had been present and knew the participants. He spoke movingly of Jesus and wept whenever he was pressed to provide more details, quickly changing the subject. Not all of the count's followers went along with the Wandering Jew theory. In view of his extraordinary scientific theories many believed that he possessed the elixir of life – an occult formula that allowed him to live for ever. In support of this they pointed out that the count never ate or drank in company, always retiring to a private room to take his refreshment. Others claimed that the count had told them that he did indeed possess the secret of eternal life and that he was far older than even his most ardent followers claimed.

One young noble reported an extraordinary conversation with one of the count's many servants. The sceptic had approached the ancient servant and said "Your master is a liar!" The man replied calmly: "I know that better than you, young sir. He tells everyone that he is four thousand years old. But I have been in his service one hundred years, and when I came the count told me he was three thousand years old. Whether he has added nine hundred years by accident or whether he lied to me I cannot say." On another occasion when the count was being pressed to provide details about a point of ancient history, he turned to his valet to prompt his memory. "Perhaps the count forgets," returned the venerable retainer, "that I have been in his service only five hundred years." If Saint Germain really did possess the elixir of life, perhaps he used it to keep some of his favourite retainers with him down the lonely centuries.

The question remains, if the Count de Saint Germain really was immortal, who was the old man who died in Eckenforde. Historians have uncovered a number of incidents in the life of the count before he reached Paris that reveal a character adept at subterfuge and changes of character. In 1745 a man was arrested in London on suspicion of being a spy for Bonnie Prince Charlie, who was then marching on Derby. A letter from Horace Walpole records the incident:

> . . . the other day they seized an odd man who goes by the name of Count Saint Germain. He has been here these two years and will not tell who he is or whence . . . He sings, plays on the violin wonderfully, composes, is mad, and not very sensible. He is called an Italian, a Spaniard, a Pole; someone that married a great fortune in Mexico, and ran away with her jewels to Constantinople; a priest, a fiddler, a vast nobleman. The Prince of Wales has had unsatisfied curiosity about him . . .

By 1755 the count was in Vienna living the life of a wealthy aristocrat. Nobody knows how such a radical change in circumstances came about. In 1760, now firmly in the confidence of the French king, Saint Germain was sent on a diplomatic mission to the Hague where he took part in secret peace negotiations with England. Reports of the count are vague and confused after this. He is reputed to have made another fortune in Holland, to have taken part in the Russo-Turkish war of 1768–74, and to have been raised to the rank of general in the Imperial Russian Army. The account of a quiet death in an obscure German town seems far from what we would expect of such a flamboyant adventurer. A man who so often changed his identity and circumstances with apparent ease, and who could disappear for years without trace, does not seem the kind of man who could be easily tracked down to a final resting place in Schleswig-Holstein. There are also the reports of meetings with the count many years after his supposed death.

Marie Antoinette received a letter from the count five years later, soon after the fall of the Bastille, warning her that France was soon to be turned on its head by a vast conspiracy. Despite his warning, the queen did not survive the revolution that swiftly followed. Madame Adhemer, a close friend of the queen's, actually met the count, who told her that he had just returned from Japan where he had uncovered the origins of a world-wide conspiracy that would bring down France. By 1870 there had been so many reported sightings of, or meetings with, the immortal count that Napoleon III, Emperor of France, ordered an official investigation. Hundreds of documents were gathered, witnesses interviewed and journals studied. Unfortunately all of this material was destroyed in a fierce fire that ripped through the Hotel de Ville the following year.

Despite his extraordinary notoriety very little physical evidence of the count remains. None of his com-positions or paintings have survived, although he was said to be a master of both arts, and only one manu-script known to be by the count is in our hands. *La Tres Sainte Trinosophie* is written in a fiendishly complex code, or perhaps an ancient forgotten language, and has so far resisted all attempts at translation.

Messiah

●●●●●●●●●●●●●●●●●●●●●●●●●●●●●●●●●●●

Was Sabbatai Levi the King of the World?

Through the centuries there have been numerous individuals who have almost, but not quite, made it into the annals of history superstardom. These are the men and women whose ambition and almost superhuman dedication to a cause have led them from humble beginnings to positions of incredible power and influence. Sometimes the tide of history is with them and sometimes it isn't. When it is they become figures of destiny, people like Napoleon, Joan of Arc or Hitler. When it isn't they are totally forgotten in latter ages despite the power they once wielded. One of the unlucky ones was a Turkish Jew named Sabbatai Levi. At one point in the seventeenth century he seemed about to become one of the most potent kings of Europe, but the tide turned against him and his incredible life was forgotten.

Sabbatai was born in the Turkish city of Smyrna (now called Izmir) in 1626. He was the son of a wealthy merchant and showed an early religious zeal that was to take over his life. At the age of sixteen he decided to undertake a permanent fast and for six years ate only the barest minimum of simple foods and drank only water. Sabbatai was twice married to girls chosen by his parents, but both marriages were unconsummated and ended in divorce. The young man's religious devotion didn't help. Apart from the constant fasting he spent hours of every day in silent prayer and contemplation, and was subject to periods of intense spiritual ecstasy and diabolical depression.

In 1648 something happened that was to alter the course of Sabbatai's life. One of many wars broke out between Poland and the Cossacks of the Ukraine. These two peoples had been at each other's throats for centuries, and the latest conflict was over Polish control of the rich farmlands of the Ukraine. A Cossack leader named Bogdan Khmelnitsky raised an army which first drove Polish landlords out of the region, and then invaded Poland itself. Both Poland and the Ukraine were home to a huge Jewish population – some large towns in the region were peopled almost entirely by Jews and every big city had a large Jewish quarter. Khmelnitsky set out not only to drive the Poles out of his country but to destroy as many Jews as possible. This was just one of dozens of persecutions or pogroms that the Jews had suffered over the centuries, and it wasn't to be the last, but it was particularly notable for its sheer scale and ferocity.

The Cossacks swept through southern Poland. Whenever they came across a Jewish community they massacred every man, woman and child without mercy. The atrocities were appalling and whole towns were left as blood-soaked, smoking ruins. Stories of the massacres reached the large Jewish populations in Turkey. Among the terrible tales that Sabbatai heard was that of a girl who had been forcibly married to a Cossack to act as his slave and concubine. The girl told her captor that she had magical powers and could not be harmed by a sword. As proof she bared her breast and invited her drunken husband to drive his blade through her. This he did, killing her stone-dead and giving her the release she had so longed for. It is estimated that as many as a 100,000 Jews lost their lives at the hands of the Cossacks.

Everyone was appalled by the stories but they had a particularly profound effect on Sabbatai. He became convinced that God was calling him to save his people. In effect, he came to believe that he was the long-awaited Messiah. One day in the synagogue Sabbatai committed the most unpardonable of sins; he stood up and shouted out the name of God. For the orthodox Jew the name of Jehovah is considered too sacred to speak out loud, and to do so in the temple was an outrage hardly to be believed. Sabbatai was announcing his presence, and it certainly worked. Like all religious fanatics Sabbatai had no trouble in assembling a crowd of devoted followers. Disturbed by this dangerous rebel in their midst, the elders of the temple banished Sabbatai and his band of followers to the town of Salonika (now in Greece and named Thessaloniki).

Once there, Sabbatai continued his outrageous behaviour and gathered more and more converts to his cause. He took to carrying a basket of fish with him which he explained was symbolic of the dawning of the Age of Pisces, when the Jews would be released from bondage and returned to the Holy Land. On one occasion he invited the local temple elders to a feast and then proceeded to carry out one of his shockingly sacrilegious stunts. Taking a scroll of the holy law in his arms, he carried it to a traditional marriage canopy that he had set up. The symbolism was clear; he was the Messiah and the law of the Jews had become his wife. Sabbatai was banished once again.

This time he took up residence in Jerusalem, the holy city itself.

In the city that Sabbatai believed was to become the seat of his kingdom on Earth, he met the two people who were to have the greatest influence on his life, a wife and a propagandist. Nathan Ashkenazi was the twenty-two-year-old son of a Jewish scholar when he first begged to be introduced to Sabbatai. The self-proclaimed Messiah was then forty years old and had been in Jerusalem for four years, slowly building up a base of devoted worshippers. As yet he had told only his trusted acolytes that he was the Messiah – a truth they had accepted without question. Nathan turned out to be Sabbatai's most valuable asset, he was a brilliant scholar and writer who knew just how to appeal to the secret wishes of the ordinary Jew. Later he was to write letters to every large Jewish community in Europe, convincing many that the Day of Judgment was at hand.

The woman who was to become Sabbatai's wife started from inauspicious beginnings. Named Sarah, she had escaped the Polish pogroms by the skin of her teeth and become a prostitute in Italy. For some reason she became convinced that she would one day marry the Messiah, and when she heard of Sabbatai she knew that her chance had come. In 1664 the future King of the World heard about Sarah and, perhaps stirred by the tales he remembered about the Polish Jews, sent twelve of his disciples to bring her from Italy. They were married in March of that year and were to remain together for the rest of their eventful lives.

With his wife and right-hand man in place, Sabbatai allowed himself to be persuaded that 1665 was the year to announce his presence to the world. The event did not go exactly as planned. News of his proclamation spread throughout Palestine and large crowds gathered, but their mood was uncertain. Sabbatai rode seven times around the city and went to assert his authority over the rabbis. Somewhat predictably they were less than impressed by his claims and banished him. The crowds turned ugly and Sabbatai was forced to make a humiliating exit. The Messiah decided it was time to return home.

As Sabbatai and his followers made the long, depressing journey back to Smyrna, they could not know the incredible impact that letters written by Nathan Ashkenazi were having all across Europe. Nathan's letters to the leaders of Jewish communities in all the major cities were read out in synagogues. Thousands were convinced by his powerful words that the Day of Judgment would soon come and that Sabbatai was the man who would lead them back to the promised land. In the streets of Amsterdam, Paris, Warsaw and Moscow, bands of Jews took to the streets and celebrated as if it was the beginning of a new world. In London the great diarist Samuel Pepys recorded that Jews were dancing in the streets and placing bets that Sabbatai would soon be King of the World. A people that had had no reason to celebrate for centuries saw their finest hour at hand. Governments and kings across the continents sat up and took notice – the Jewish population of Europe was several million strong; who knew what would happen if these quiet, disparate people were suddenly united under a visionary leader.

Not everyone was so pleased by the rise and rise of Sabbatai. Ever since he had stood up in the synagogue at Smyrna and blasphemed the name of Jehovah, the new Messiah's theology had drifted further and further from the orthodox message. Like many charismatic spiritual leaders before and since, Sabbatai preached the overturn of virtually every established religious taboo. In an era when men and women were strictly segregated in Jewish society, the Sabbataians believed that men and women were equal and should mix freely, and when they said freely they meant really freely. Incest and promiscuity were openly practised and many of Sabbatai's followers indulged in ritualized self-mutilation, which often involved the sin of public nudity. Sabbatai himself proclaimed that divorced women, or those accused of adultery, should enjoy the same rights as everyone else – wasn't his own wife a former prostitute?

The height of the Sabbataian's frenzy came when their leader announced his intention of visiting Constantinople, the imperial capital of the Ottoman Empire. As in other cities there was a sense of impending liberation among the large Jewish population. The sultan, Mehmet IV, was more than a little alarmed, especially when his closest advisers warned him that Sabbatai was an ambitious trickster who wanted only one thing: to depose the Sultan and take the throne for himself. Once again Sabbatai was quite unaware of the chaos his impending arrival was causing and was surprised when, even before he had got off the boat, he was arrested by soldiers and taken to prison. The Messiah was lucky to escape with his life. Fortunately, his followers in Constantinople managed to bribe enough of the right people and his execution was cancelled.

Released from prison, Sabbatai was installed in a luxurious palace in Gallipoli where he was allowed to continue to receive visitors and preach his message.

One of these visitors turned out to be of momentous importance, although Sabbatai saw him only as an annoying old man who insisted on arguing theology with him. The old man, a Polish scholar named Nehemiah ha-Kolen, left his meeting with Sabbatai feeling insulted and went straight to the sultan to denounce the Messiah as a fraud and a revolutionary. The sultan's fears were reawakened and he summoned Sabbatai to his palace.

Standing before the ruler of one of the richest and most powerful empires in the world on that day in September 1666, Sabbatai faced a pivotal moment in his life. The sultan demanded that he convert to Islam there and then, or be executed on the spot as a traitor. Had Sabbatai rebuffed the sultan he would have been killed and made an instant martyr at the height of his fame and popularity. It's tempting to imagine what would have happened. The Jewish community was on a knife-edge of tension and religious fervour, the death of their Messiah could have sparked the first Jewish revolt since the time of Simon Bar Kochba in the second century AD. But it was not to be. Inexplicably Sabbatai bowed to the will of the sultan and accepted a new name and a new religion. His followers were stunned; the man they had hoped would lead them to a new and better life had betrayed them in an instant. What had happened to the twenty-year-old zealot who had sworn to free his people?

Sabbatai had come a long way since his youth in Smyrna. He had seen the world and grown a little wiser for it. The failure at Jerusalem had been more of a blow than anyone realized and the ease with which he had been captured by the sultan's troops did little to encourage him. Perhaps he had come to realize a long time before that he was no Messiah, that at the moment of truth his nerve would fail. For years he had enjoyed the adulation of his followers, the love of his wife and he had wanted for nothing. Somewhere he had lost the will that had driven him as a young man, but he had put himself in a position from which it was impossible to stand down. When the chance came to get out and retire to a comfortable life, he grabbed it with both hands.

Sabbatai lived in Constantinople on a generous pension for another six years. Occasionally his old, fiery spirit would return and he would do something to outrage the rabbis and embarrass the sultan. Eventually he was sent to a remote village in Albania where he lived on for another four years. Surprisingly, a number of his followers stood by him to the end, including Nathan. They convinced themselves that their master's conversion to Islam was a riddle or parable, the meaning of which would one day be revealed to the world. As an old man Sabbatai would sometimes climb the hills around his humble village and proclaim to the world that he was indeed the Messiah, but nobody was listening any more.

The Great Impostor

•••••••••••••••••••••••••••••••••

Ferdinand Waldo Demara – man of a thousand faces

The world is full of conmen and scam artists; trickery and deception as a means of obtaining money is a method as old as the rather more direct club over the head. The vast majority of conmen are cruel and mercenary individuals for whom money is the only object, and the natural instinct of most people to trust a friendly face is a meal ticket to be ruthlessly exploited. These are criminals just as heartless as the burglar who climbs in through your window and ransacks your house. For some people, however, trickery, deception and the projection of a false identity are a kind of compulsion that has little or nothing to do with gaining wealth. One such man was Ferdinand Waldo Demara, a man of a thousand faces, also known as the Great Impostor.

Waldo Demara was born in Lawrence, Massachusetts, in 1921. From the start he found it almost impossible to fit into patterns of behaviour expected of him, although his whole life can be seen as a search for a structured environment where he could fit in. At the age of sixteen Waldo dropped out of high school and ran away from home. His first attempt at a new life took him to a Trappist monastery where he quickly gained a reputation for studiousness and devotion to his duties. After two years he could stand the frugal monk's lifestyle no more and left the monastery to join the US Army. Almost immediately he realized that military life was not going to suit him either.

Waldo was stationed at Kessler Field in Biloxi, Mississippi. Although a disciplined life was what he craved, the young Private Demara, now aged eighteen, couldn't stand the reality of discipline. His life as a perpetual impostor began here. Noticing that the orderlies who assigned troops to their units seemed to avoid all the worst jobs around the camp, Waldo decided to become one. Typically he also decided to short cut the tedious business of earning the status he desired. Instead he simply made himself an orderly's armband, carried a clipboard and took on the duties without anyone noticing. Waldo had always been a bright kid able to pick up new ideas and procedures almost instantly. Coupled with an acting streak a mile wide, this talent enabled Waldo to take on any persona and look as if he knew exactly what he was doing. Soon the meagre benefits of the orderly persona tarnished for Waldo and he decided it was time to get out.

One day he was invited to the home of a more senior soldier. Noticing the military paraphernalia of citations, medals and other documents, Waldo was struck with an idea. Returning one night, he broke into the house and made off with enough military regalia to establish a new identity for himself as an experienced and respected soldier. Wearing his new persona like a glove, Waldo felt drawn to return to the Trappist order. He was accepted into a different monastery from the one he had entered at the age of eighteen and, as usual, made a great impression. Unfortunately, however, a student from Waldo's original monastery happened to recognize him and he was asked to leave after only one week.

In 1942, just after the Japanese bombed Pearl Harbor, Demara enlisted in the US Navy. He received first-aid training at the Hospital School which awoke in him a lifelong interest in medicine. When he applied for advanced training, however, his lack of educational achievements told against him and he was turned down. Waldo resorted to his usual methods. He stole credentials belonging to a Dr Robert French, walked off the base and took a job as a science teacher at a Catholic boys school. Again his ability to grasp new disciplines served him well as he taught himself each new subject the week before he had to teach it to his students. Eventually the abbot got around to checking his references and the game was up. Demara stole a car and headed for Chicago.

Once again he was drawn to the church. Although he had been born a Catholic Demara had already "converted" to the religion twice, and now he decided to become an ordained priest. Faced with years of study and a return to a monk-like lifestyle, however, Demara changed his mind and, using his stolen doctor's credentials, secured a position as dean of the School of Philosophy at Gannon College in Pennsylvania. As usual he tried to go too far too fast and made a number of suggestions for improving the college that alienated the school's management. From Chicago he made his way to Washington where he ran a psychological counselling centre and then held the post of deputy sheriff. Entering the law enforcement profession had been a mistake. His false identity was uncovered and he was arrested. The most serious charge hanging over him was desertion from the navy in time of war, an offence that could have cost him his life. Demara defended himself and received only an eighteen-month sentence.

On his release from prison Demara knew exactly what he was going to do. He enrolled as a law student in Boston and stuck it out for a whole year before debunking to Maine to teach biology at a small college. As before, his ambitious plans were his undoing. After the college became a university, largely thanks to his efforts, he was disappointed to find that he was not going to be promoted. In a fit of pique he left the college, but not before he had stolen copies of medical credentials belonging to a Dr Joseph Cyr.

In 1951 newspapers published stories about a "super" doctor who had saved countless lives on active service in the Canadian Navy. The miracle doctor was of course Dr Cyr, aka Waldo Demara. After leaving Maine, Waldo had joined the Canadian Navy and, using his false medical qualifications, got himself appointed chief medical officer on board the destroyer *Cayuga*. It was in this new role that Waldo faced his greatest challenge yet. The *Cayuga* was stationed off the coast of Korea, a country then in the midst of a bitter civil war that had drawn in the United States, Great Britain and a host of other western nations. Waldo found himself called on to perform medical procedures on desperately wounded soldiers that would have tested the skill of any qualified physician. On one occasion he worked through the night operating on a boatload of wounded South Korean soldiers. Fortified with rum and prayer, Waldo performed a series of dangerous and difficult operations using instruments that he had never even seen before. None of his patients died. Later he was called on to remove a bullet-pierced lung, a procedure he carried out flawlessly by referring to a medical journal he happened to have lying around.

It was Demara's greatest triumph, but it was also his undoing. When the real Dr Cyr read the accounts of his exploits in the Canadian Navy, he reported it to the authorities and Waldo was sent back to Canada to face trial. The navy found itself in a difficult position. Not only was "Dr Cyr" a hero, he had actually saved the lives of numerous servicemen. Eventually he was simply discharged from the service for having joined under a false name. To have tried Demara for faking his qualifications would have made the navy look bad and, considering his success, would have been difficult to prove.

Never one to be disheartened, Demara moved to Texas, changed his name to Ben Jones, and walked into a job as a prison warder in the maximum security wing of Huntsville Jail. In the meantime he had sold his story to *Life* magazine for a considerable sum. Contact with the media proved to be a mistake once again. A prisoner read the article and pointed it out to the governor. The state had no choice but to sack Jones, despite the fact that he had been one of their best staff members. The noose of recognition was growing ever tighter. Back in Maine, Demara ran a school for a time, until he was arrested again. All charges were dropped when parents rallied round and defended the excellent work he had done. By 1956 he was a teacher at a high school in Maine under the name Martin Godgart, but by now the game was up.

Everywhere Demara went people had heard of him or seen his face in the papers. In 1960 a book about his life entitled *The Great Impostor* was published and became a national best-seller. Soon after, it was made into a movie starring Tony Curtis. All avenues were closed.

The great impostor could be no one but Waldo Demara. In the late 1970s Demara turned up again, as a properly ordained minister, under his own name, and working as a hospital chaplain in Anaheim, California. He died in 1982 at the age of sixty.

What had driven this man to take on so many different personalities? He was sociable, well liked, intelligent and strong-willed; there seems no reason that he couldn't have made a great success of his life. The detective who arrested Demara after his stint as a high school teacher in Maine commented that he was a man who just wanted too much out of life. His new identities gave him the opportunity to start again with a clean slate, to leave behind difficulties and responsibilities and start over. Although this sounds like a reasonable assessment of the man's character, Waldo himself was quoted as saying, "Every time I take on a new identity, a piece of me dies."

Demara may have started out as an impatient young man eager to grab opportunities without having to work for them, but as the years passed the need to identity-swap must have become an irresistible compulsion. Each time he took the next leap into a new life he got deeper into a web of lies and left the reality of who he was and where he came from a little further behind. His desire to belong is evident throughout his adventures. Time and again Waldo tried to get into institutions that would provide him with a strong, supporting framework for his life; the military, the church, medicine or academia. But each time he tried he was disappointed by the experience, or frightened off by the responsibility, and bailed out. For all the excitement of his life he was, in the end, a broken man; without real identity, without a history and without a place to turn to.

The Skipton Witch

••

Misunderstood genius of the sixteenth century?

The middle of the sixteenth century was not a good time to be suspected as a witch. In those days the merest hint of supernatural powers in a woman could quickly lead to terrible torture and immolation at the stake. Yet this was the era in which England's greatest seer, Mother Shipton, lived and thrived. Mother Shipton was famed throughout the land and in Yorkshire, where she lived, she was feared and respected as a witch with incredible powers. Despite the obvious dangers, it was a reputation she clearly enjoyed and did her best to live up to. Mother Shipton wasn't worried – she had foreseen her own death and knew that it would come to her at home in the peace of her own bed and not in the flames of an executioner's pyre.

In 1530 the great Yorkshire witch made one of her startling predictions about a notable figure of the day. She said that the "Mitred Peacock", Cardinal Wolsey – the most powerful churchman of his day – would one day try to escape to York after a falling out with King Henry VIII, but that he would die before he entered the city's gates. Wolsey's relationship with the king was already suffering because the cardinal had failed to persuade the pope to allow Henry to divorce his first wife, Catherine of Aragon. Outraged at this prediction made by a simple countrywoman, Cardinal Wolsey set out for York to prove her wrong and to have her burned as a witch.

Wolsey sent three spies, all noblemen, ahead of him to find out more about Mother Shipton. When they arrived at her house with a local guide they were shocked to discover that the old woman had been expecting them and had provided oat cakes and ale for the occasion. With their cover blown by the witch's uncanny second sight the men asked why she had predicted that Wolsey would never reach York. She reminded them that her prediction had been that Wolsey would see York, but never enter it. Annoyed by what seemed like petty word-play they told her that the cardinal would surely have her burned when he arrived. Mother Shipton was not worried, she threw a linen napkin on to the fire and said, "If this cloth burns then so shall I." Flames licked all around the cloth but, after several minutes, the witch removed it from the fire and showed that it had not even been scorched.

A short while later, Wolsey and his entourage reached Yorkshire. One evening they halted just eight miles from the city, intending to enter in grand procession the next day. Wolsey could see the towers of the minster and the city walls across the flat country of the vale of York, and felt confident that he had cheated Mother Shipton's prophecy. The next day, as Wolsey prepared to enter the city, a troop of soldiers rode up and arrested the cardinal on charges of treason. As he was taken away the churchman looked back at the gates he had so nearly reached and realized he was doomed. He died on the way to face trial in London. Mother Shipton had been proved right again, as she had been so many times in the past. There seemed no limit to the woman's powers.

Mother Shipton was born Ursula Southiel in the town of Knaresborough in July of 1488. Her mother, Agatha Southiel, was an unmarried seventeen-year-old. Many strange stories are told about the birth of Ursula Southiel. According to popular local legend she was born on the moors after her mother had been cast out of the town for consorting with the devil. The story goes that Agatha Southiel was an orphan and beggar who had fallen in love with a handsome gentleman on a black horse. The man turned out to be the devil who, once he had made her pregnant, left her to die on the moors as she gave birth to his daughter. Another version says that Agatha survived the birth, but later entered a convent after the child began to show signs of its unnatural origins. Whatever the truth might be, the baby Ursula grew up an orphan like her mother.

For a few years Ursula lived with a foster mother in the town, but as she grew from a baby to a child she quickly developed the powerful personality and menacing manner that was to serve her well throughout her life. Her poor foster mother was terrified of the child, who would growl like an animal when told off, and seemed to be surrounded by strange phenomena. Objects would whirl around the cottage as the unearthly Ursula sat in the middle of the floor chuckling. The walls would throb as if from a giant heartbeat, and invisible hands would rip and grope at the beleaguered foster mother. Eventually she could take no more and sent the child away to school.

At first her new environment seemed to suit Ursula well. Her teachers were astounded at her intelligence and quickness, and she seemed to have a wealth of knowledge that did not fit at all with her background as a poor child from a simple country town. Soon, however, the other children began to taunt her for being an orphan and the offspring of the devil. Many of them came to regret this as she would set evil spirits loose on her tormentors to beat them and tear their clothes. The disruption was too much, however, and Ursula was moved from school to school until eventually there was nowhere for her to go, and she was left to fend for herself. Ursula didn't seem to mind, she never showed any sign of fear or loneliness and set out to take on the world. Within a short time she was married to a man named Tobias Shipton and the couple moved to the town of Skipton where Ursula lived out the rest of her life.

Now a respectable married woman in a town where nobody knew her name, Ursula Shipton seems to have taken on a more gentle character. She turned her powers to the art of prophecy and healing and there are no reports of her harming or deliberately terrifying anyone in this new phase of her life. She was constantly in demand by local people who wanted to know if their crops would do well, if their husband's illness would clear up or if their sweetheart would marry them, but Mother Shipton's mind was on greater things. She was clearly a highly intelligent woman and kept herself well informed of political developments at home and abroad. When Henry VIII invaded France in 1513, Mother Shipton had already predicted it as she foresaw the subsequent English victory at the Battle of the Spurs. When Wolsey's three spies visited her many years later she had predictions for them all.

To the Duke of Suffolk she revealed that in the future he would become as low as she. The puzzled Duke probably thought no more about it until twenty-four years later, when he laid his head on the executioner's block to be beheaded for treason. Lord Percy received the news that his head would one day decorate the gates of

York and then be taken to France, without a flicker of emotion. In 1572 his head was indeed impaled on a pole over one of the gates of York and was later stolen by a French Catholic. Lord Darcy was not worried when Mother Shipton told him that his "great gun" would not save him from death in battle. He was executed for treason after the failure of an uprising against the king in 1536, when he relied on artillery to win him a battle.

Mother Shipton, prophetess. From Caulfield's Wonderful Museum of Remarkable Portraits, London 1794.

Many of Mother Shipton's prophecies about events that took place in her own lifetime, or shortly after, can be explained as the astute predictions of an intelligent political commentator. She knew that England was entering a period of upheaval as Henry VIII broke away from the Catholic church, and foresaw that many nobles would lose their lives. Her famous prediction about the Spanish Armada of 1588 can be seen in the same light. Not only was Spain the most powerful Catholic country of the time, its rulers sworn to defend the Catholic church, but rivalry between England and Spain over territory in the recently discovered New World was inevitable. It didn't take a huge leap of the imagination to foresee a Spanish fleet being sent to crush the English throne.

Politics was not Mother Shipton's only interest however. Like many seers she was visited by tremendous visions of events far beyond her own era. Many of these prophecies, which she recorded in clever rhymes, seem to predict things that wouldn't happen until centuries later. One of the most famous is a vision of a world not unlike our own.

> And now a word, in uncouth rhyme
> Of what shall be in future time
> Then upside down the world shall be
> And gold found at the root of tree
> All England's sons that plough the land
> Shall oft be seen with Book in hand
> The poor shall now great wisdom know
> Great houses stand in farflung vale
> All covered o'er with snow and hail
> A carriage without horse will go
> Disaster fill the world with woe.

In London, Primrose Hill shall be
In centre hold a Bishop's See
Around the world men's thoughts will fly
Quick as the twinkling of an eye.
And water shall great wonders do
How strange. And yet it shall come true.
Through towering hills proud men shall ride
No horse or ass move by his side.

Beneath the water, men shall walk
Shall ride, shall sleep, shall even talk.
And in the air men shall be seen
In white and black and even green
A great man then, shall come and go
For prophecy declares it so.

One can sense a kind of longing in many of Mother Shipton's prophetic verses. Apart from the startling references to flying machines, horseless carriages, worldwide communications and submarines, there is the hope of an age when "The poor shall know great wisdom" and "England's sons . . . Shall oft be seen with Book in hand". Perhaps Mother Shipton's prophecies were more wishes than visions of the future. She was clearly an intelligent woman trapped in an era when she had no hope of receiving a good education and making her mark in the world. The only "career" with influence open to a woman with such an acute mind was as a witch or seer – a course she followed with relish despite the danger of being associated with apparently satanic powers. A clue to her feelings can be found in part of another of her strange poems.

> *For in those wondrous far off days*
> *The women shall adopt a craze*
> *To dress like men, and trousers wear*
> *And to cut off their locks of hair*
> *They'll ride astride with brazen brow*
> *As witches do on broomstick now.*

Mother Shipton's writings attracted their fair share of "revisers" and "interpreters" after her death. The most notorious of these was Charles Hindley, who, in the mid-nineteenth century, added his own verses to the words of Mother Shipton. Among his additions were the apocalyptic lines:

> *When the world to an end shall come*
> *In eighteen hundred and ninety-one.*

The reputation of the Skipton witch suffered as a result of this foolish meddling with her words. No doubt she saw it coming because she made a prediction which, unusually, included a specific date some time after 1891.

> *In nineteen hundred and twenty-six*
> *Build houses light of straw and sticks.*
> *For then shall mighty wars be planned*
> *And fire and sword shall sweep the land.*
> *When pictures seem alive with movements free*
> *When boats like fishes swim beneath the sea,*
> *When men like birds shall scour the sky*
> *Then half the world, deep drenched in blood shall*
> *   die.*

Mother Shipton died peacefully at home in 1561. In this, as in every thing else she had seen during her seventy-three years, she was proved to be absolutely right.

Kaspar Hauser

●●●●●●●●●●●●●●●●●●●●●●●●●●●●●●●●●●●

The legendary boy from nowhere

> *He neither knows who he is nor where he came from, for it was only at Nuremberg that he came into the world. He always lived in a hole, where he sat on straw on the ground; he never heard a sound nor saw a vivid light. He awoke and slept and awoke again; when he awoke he found a loaf of bread and a pitcher of water beside him. Sometimes the water tasted bad, and then he fell asleep again, and when he woke up he found a clean shirt on; he never saw the face of the man who came to him.*

These words, written in 1828, were part of the first public statement about the mysterious boy known as Kaspar Hauser. Ever since his sudden and mysterious appearance in the German market town of Nuremberg, this strange and unearthly lad had been at the centre of a whirl of speculation and rumour. The mystery was to become deeper still and has never been solved to this day.

It all began on the morning of 26 May 1828 – a holiday when farmers from miles around came to sell, buy and enjoy themselves in the market square. A cobbler named George Weichmann noticed a strange youth wandering into town from the direction of New

Gate. The lad looked large and sturdy but was hobbling badly and seemed to be utterly terrified and bemused by everything around him. Weichmann offered to help but the startled boy seemed unable to speak, all he could do was hold out a letter addressed to "Captain of the 4th Squadron, 6th Cavalry Regiment, Nuremberg". Intrigued and concerned for the boy's health the cobbler took him to the house of Captain Wessenig and persuaded the servants to let them wait for his return.

In the captain's house the speechless boy was offered food and drink. He consumed a loaf of bread like a wild animal but refused to touch meat. Given a flagon of beer he seemed fascinated by the colour and lustre of the cup but completely ignored its contents. Other everyday things about the room seemed to hold an odd fascination for the strange lad. He was terrified of a large pendulum clock and shied away from it as if it were a fearful animal. When he saw a burning candle he let out a shriek of delighted surprise and immediately reached out to scoop up the flame. By now a number of servants had gathered round and were seeking to produce still more bizarre reactions from their guest. A ball that was bounced across the room and landed on the boy's lap was greeted with glee and stroked and petted as if it were a living thing. At no point did he speak an intelligible word other than to say "Don't know" in response to every question.

Eventually Captain Wessenig returned home and was introduced to the boy, who eagerly handed him the letter he had been clutching on the street. The letter actually consisted of two notes, each written by a different hand, and were consistently badly spelled and grammatically awkward.

The First Letter – undated

Honoured Captain
I send you a lad who wished to serve his king in the Army. He was brought to me on October 7th, 1812. I am but a poor labourer with children of my own. His mother asked me to bring up the boy, and so I thought I would raise him as my own son. Since then, I have never let him go one step outside the house, so no one knows where he was raised. He, himself, does not know the name of the place or what it is. You may question him, honoured Captain, but he will not be able to tell you where I live. I brought him out at night. He cannot find his way back. He has not a penny for I have nothing myself. If you will not keep him, you must strike him dead or hang him.

The Second Letter – dated October 1812

This child has been baptized. His name is Kaspar; you must give him his second name yourself. I ask you to take care of him. His father was a cavalry soldier. When he is seventeen, take him to Nuremberg, to the Sixth Cavalry Regiment; his father belonged to it. I beg you to keep him until he is seventeen. He was born on April 30th, 1812. I am a poor girl; I can't take care of him. His father is dead.

Wessenig was less than impressed by the letters and, regarding the boy as an obvious imbecile or hoaxer, he had Kaspar removed to the police station. At the station Sergeant Wust made a detailed description of the boy. He had been persuaded to write his name on a sheet of paper but still responded to all further questions with

"Don't know". Wust described Kaspar as a broad-shouldered youth of about seventeen or eighteen years of age. He had light brown hair and blue eyes. He was found to be wearing odd clothes that clearly did not belong to him. His trousers and shirt were badly worn and far too large, his shoes were so tight that his toes had forced their way through the ends, causing bruising and blisters that made walking very difficult. Wust also noted that, apart from the blisters, the boy's hands and feet were smooth and obviously not used to hard manual labour. Nothing on his person provided the slightest clue to his identity – apart from the two letters.

As a temporary measure Kaspar was kept in a police cell. The jailer remarked that he seemed far more at home there than anywhere else. Kaspar would sit stock-still in the dark, as if he hardly dared to move. His ability to remain motionless for hours on end astonished the jailer, who was used to his charges fidgeting with boredom and frustration. He also noted that, when he did move around, the lack of light seemed to present no more problem to him than it would a nocturnal animal. It later emerged that Kaspar's senses were supernaturally acute. Not only could he see incredibly well in the dark, his hearing was tremendously acute and he could identify people, plants and animals by scent alone. News of the mysterious prisoner in the town's jail spread quickly and a small throng of people gathered daily outside his cell to peer in at him through the window. Kaspar learned to speak and write amazingly quickly – or perhaps just remembered how to do these things – and within a few weeks a statement was issued to a curious public in the form of a pamphlet entitled "Bulletin Number One – Concerning the Child of Nuremberg".

Police interviews with Kaspar seemed to indicate that he had been the victim of appalling, but perhaps unintentional, cruelty. He remembered nothing other than a dark, lonely room before the time he appeared in the city, and he had no idea how he had come to be there nor how he came to leave it. Kaspar had become famous throughout Europe by this time and the police were keen to be seen to be doing something. Agents made a massive search of Bavaria looking for his place of childhood imprisonment, and thousands of leaflets were circulated asking for anyone with information to come forward. No one did, despite the substantial reward on offer. Eventually, with no reason to keep him in custody, the police released Kaspar into the custody of Professor George Friedrich Daumer, a distinguished educationalist who had become fascinated by the case.

With Professor Daumer, Kaspar experienced perhaps the first happy times of his life. Daumer dismissed the idea that his charge was an imbecile and set about to see how much he could be taught. Kaspar responded marvellously. His vocabulary and writing skills progressed apace and he took to drawing with an enthusiasm and skill that stunned his guardian. In 1829, Daumer helped Kaspar write his autobiography. Although eagerly awaited, it answered few of the questions on everybody's lips, and none of the big ones. Kaspar simply had no idea who he was or where he came from, beyond the image of the dark room where he had apparently spent the first sixteen years of his life. Of the man who had kept him there he could provide few details. Kaspar apparently had no hatred for the man, he only remembered being struck once, for being noisy.

Suddenly, in October of that same year the Kaspar Hauser mystery took a shocking and disturbing turn.

Kaspar was found in the cellar of Professor Daumer's house spreadeagled on the floor and bleeding profusely from a head wound. Once he had recovered from the shock, an ashen-faced Kaspar reported that he had been in the cellar when a tall man, dressed in black and wearing a black mask, had jumped him from the shadows and slashed him with a knife. The city was scandalized, Kaspar was a much loved, if occasionally ridiculed figure, and nobody could understand who would want to harm him. Two police officers were assigned to protect the boy day and night. Eighteen months later, in May of 1831, a second mysterious attack took place. One of his bodyguards rushed into Kaspar's upstairs room when he heard a gunshot ring out. Again the boy was found on the floor with a bleeding head wound. Kaspar claimed that he had been climbing on a chair when he had fallen and knocked a pistol off the wall. The pistol had gone off and the bullet had just grazed his head. Some suspected that this might have been a suicide attempt.

By now Kaspar had been moved to the home of his new guardian, Anselm Ritter von Feuerbach, who had begun to develop dark suspicions about the true identity of his innocent young ward. In May of 1833 von Feuerbach died suddenly from a paralytic stroke. He had been in the middle of compiling a detailed dossier on the Kaspar Hauser case, which was soon discovered and published all over Europe. Entitled "Example of a Crime Against the Life of a Soul of a Man", the report made startling reading. It had been suggested before that Kaspar might be the illegitimate son of a powerful noble, and that his years of imprisonment had been an attempt to keep him hidden until all danger of a scandal had passed. This idea went some way towards explaining the odd comment in the letter provided by Kaspar's first "guardian" that ". . . I have never let him go one step outside the house, so no one knows where he was raised". Von Feuerbach, however, doubted that anybody would go to such trouble to conceal an illegitimate child – they were hardly uncommon among the upper classes. More likely, von Feuerbach argued, the child was the legitimate heir to a powerful position and that he was kept out of the way until an impostor could take up his inheritance. The report concluded that the only position that would have warranted such an elaborate ploy must be a royal one. Von Feuerbach was dead before he had a chance to elaborate further, if he ever intended to.

A few months later the mystery took its final, tragic twist. Kaspar was staying with a English aristocrat who had taken an interest in his case when, on the afternoon of 11 December 1833, he staggered home from a walk in the park with a deep stab-wound in his abdomen. He was clearly seriously hurt but managed to gasp out that he had been stabbed by a man in the park. Captain Hickel, who had been charged with protecting Kaspar, raced to the park hoping to find some sign of the assailant. All he found were Kaspar's own bloodstained footprints in the snow. Later that day, as Kaspar lay dying from the wound which had pierced his stomach and heart, he told a strange tale about the events of the day. He said that he had gone to the park at the invitation of a man who had contacted him via a servant earlier in the day. Once there, he was approached by a tall man with black whiskers and a black cloak who asked him if he was Kaspar Hauser. When Kaspar answered that he was, the man suddenly stuck him with a long sharp instrument and ran off. Kaspar couldn't explain why there were no tracks other than his own in the snow. Six days later Kaspar slipped into a coma and died soon after. The assailant from the park was never identified or apprehended.

In the 170 years since his death Kaspar Hauser's story has been retold, re-interpreted and re-examined countless times. The bare fact of his sudden appearance as a seventeen-year-old with the innocence of a new-born is fascinating enough, but the strange and eventually fatal sequence of mysterious attacks that seem to have descended on him without reason make the mystery one of the most compelling ever. Many writers have subscribed to the theory that he was indeed a disinherited heir to some powerful noble title. There seems to be no other rational explanation for his imprisonment. Yet if this was the reason, why keep him alive at all, and why release him just as he reached an age when he could legally claim such an inheritance? The letters he carried when he was first "found" seem to indicate that somebody cared for him as a child, even if their methods were a little odd. It was widely claimed at the time that Kaspar was no more than a hoaxer seeking attention and that his injuries were all self-inflicted to gain extra sympathy. The doctors who performed the autopsy claimed that the wound that killed him could not have been self-inflicted, but doctors have been wrong before, and the fact that there were no tracks in the park other than Kaspar's is a puzzling piece of evidence. Whatever the truth perhaps the monument that marks the place he received his fatal wound in the Hofgarten at Ansbach sums up the Kaspar Hauser story best. It reads "On this place for mysterious reasons one mysterious figure was murdered by another mysterious figure".

Prester John

●●●●●●●●●●●●●●●●●●●●●●●●●●●●●●●●

Christian king of the Orient?

In 1145 Bishop Otto of Bavaria met Bishop Hugh of
Syria to discuss the latest news from the Holy Land. As
both men knew, the situation was grave. The great
hopes of the Christian crusades against the Islamic
empire had been dashed. Although Christian knights
had a foothold in Palestine and had managed to take
the city of Jerusalem, they faced a powerful enemy that
surrounded them on every side. It seemed doubtful
that the Christian strongholds, manned by fanatical
bands of warrior monks such as the Templars, would
hold out for long if the "Saracens", as the Moslems
were known, were to launch an assault. But Bishop
Hugh also had good news, for he had heard an incredible story that promised hope for the beleaguered
Christian army. The story that Bishop Hugh told was to
become the basis for one of the most enduring legends
of medieval Europe, and a fascinating puzzle for later
historians.

Bishop Otto learned that a powerful Christian
monarch from India, known as Presbyter Iohannes,
was on the verge of crushing the Islamic empire and
sweeping to the aid of Jerusalem. Hugh told of a great
battle that had taken place in which this mysterious
lord from the East had crushed a combined force of
Medes, Persians and Assyrians and taken the city of

Egbattana (now known as Hamadan). The conquering army had marched on into the Saracens' territory and only halted when they reached the mighty River Tigris. Unable to convey his army across the floodwaters, Presbyter Iohannes had marched north and camped on the banks waiting for the river to freeze over; when it did he would resume his push on Jerusalem.

Bishop Otto conveyed what he had heard to the pope, and the story spread throughout Christian Europe. The name of the mysterious eastern monarch became simplified to Prester John; Presbyter means priest and Iohannes is a German equivalent of John. For centuries there had been rumours and half-forgotten tales about Christian communities that had thrived in the Middle and Far East. The apostle St Thomas was said to have travelled far into the East and converted many of the peoples he encountered. Even the best-educated and well-travelled Europeans of the time knew next to nothing about the mysterious East. For centuries the hostility of the Islamic peoples of the Middle East and North Africa had prevented Europeans from travelling extensively into Asia or Africa. European maps of the time show both continents as one vast, shapeless land mass inhabited by mythical beasts and lost tribes. It was a temptingly plausible idea that one of the communities visited by St Thomas had grown into a powerful empire and was now on the verge of sweeping to Europe's aid against the hated Saracens.

Despite the expectations of imminent liberation from the East, no shining army of Christian knights materialized. Then, in 1165, something happened which completely re-animated the excitement of twenty years before. A letter, addressed jointly to the

Emperor Manuel I of Byzantium and the Holy Roman Emperor Frederick Barbarossa, and apparently from Prester John himself, appeared in Europe. The letter opened with fraternal greetings from one Christian king to another and reassurances that the kingdom of Prester John was a reality. Much of the text describes the wonders of the Indian kingdom – a land of free-flowing milk and honey; home to wild hares the size of sheep and other incredible creatures such as the unicorn and the centaur; populated with races such as the beautiful and fierce race of warrior women known as the Amazons; and inexhaustible mines of gold and precious stones. Most fabulous of all was the royal palace of Prester John himself: 30,000 men and women were said to reside there and banquets were held every night on tables of pure gold or emerald.

These claims sound so obviously fantastic to the modern reader, but they were surprisingly plausible to the medieval one. Hampered by an almost complete ignorance about the lands to the east of Europe, and steeped in a combination of ancient, half-remembered Greek and Roman myths, influential figures of the day were all too ready to believe. Copies of the letters were translated into every European language and became the talk of archbishops' dinners, royal feasts and common taverns. The letter was clearly a fake, quite possibly there were several letters written over a period of several years and later conflated into one, but whoever wrote them sparked of one of the most important eras in European and world history. The epic period of exploration and expansion which saw Europeans discover new lands, circle the globe and reach every part of the world really began with the search for the kingdom of Prester John.

In 1221 the by now familiar reports of a Christian king winning victories in the East began to surface again. This time they proved to be at least half right. A mighty ruler was indeed overrunning the Moslems in the East, but he was no Christian, he was Ghengis Khan. The Khan's million-strong army swept all before it, and soon reached the borders of Europe. Suddenly Christendom was faced with a threat that made the menace of the Islamic powers seem like child's play. Fortunately Ghengis had no intention of conquering western Europe and his victories allowed Europeans to travel east for the first time in centuries. With Mongol horsemen keen to encourage trade and patrolling the ancient silk-route all the way from China to the Danube, European travellers and traders leapt at the chance and headed for the mysterious East. Among the first were missionaries who hoped to convert the Mongols and to locate the kingdom of Prester John. Those who survived returned with incredible tales.

In 1245 a Franciscan monk named John de Carpini made an amazing 6000-mile round trip into deepest Mongolia to visit the camp of the Great Khan. In 1253 William of Rubruck made a similar journey and in 1270 the most famous of all travellers to the East, the Venetian Marco Polo, made it all the way to China. Both Marco Polo and William of Rubruck heard a story that shed some light on the mysterious Prester John. It was said that Ghengis Khan had become ruler of his people after defeating his predecessor, a Christian named Ung Khan. Other sources have since confirmed that there was a Christian ruler in central Asia around the year 1000. Other travellers speculated that the conquests of Ghengis had driven Prester John or his descendants out of that part of Asia and into Abyssinia, or Ethiopia as it is known today.

Europeans at least knew that there were Christian peoples living in Ethiopia, pilgrims from there arrived in Jerusalem regularly, but as to what wonders the country may hold they were as much in the dark as they had been about the Mongol lands a century earlier. One man, inspired by the search for Prester John's land, did more than any other to push back the boundaries of Europe's knowledge of the world. Third son of King João I of Portugal, Prince Henry, known as Henry the Navigator, equipped vessels to sail further south along the African coast than any European had been since the days of the Roman Empire. Prince Henry's explorers gradually penetrated further and further until, in 1488, Bartholomew Dias finally rounded the southern tip of Africa. It had taken almost a century, but the way was open for a sea route to the East. At the same time that Dias and his fellow explorer, Vasco de Gama, were trying to reach Ethiopia by sea, Portugal was sending daring agents to try and penetrate Moslem lands and reach Prester John's supposed kingdom over land. Many died in the attempt and the few who did manage the incredible journey were held captive in Ethiopia and never allowed to leave.

It wasn't until 1527 that a Portuguese mission made a successful trip to Ethiopia and returned with a detailed account. The emissaries saw many incredible sights, but they did not find Prester John. Ethiopia was certainly Christian and had been since soon after the death of Christ. It had held out against the advance of the Moslems thanks to a ring of almost impenetrable mountains that surrounded it. The Ethiopians built incredible churches entirely hewn from the living rock and carried out annual baptisms. But they called their leader emperor and had never heard the name Prester John. The Portuguese were bitterly disappointed. Almost four hundred years after the legend had begun it seemed that Prester John, if he had ever existed, would never be found. Times were changing fast, however, and nobody else really cared any more. The Portuguese had opened up brand new and highly lucrative trade routes to the East and the vast new continents of the Americas had just been discovered. The Moslem empire had long since stopped expanding and nobody needed a knight in shining armour to ride in from the east.

Although Prester John and his fabulously wealthy kingdom were never found, scholars have remained fascinated by just who or what sparked off the legend in the first place. Our knowledge of the history of the vast central Asian territories is sketchy and poorly documented at best, and there are tantalizing clues that a powerful Christian empire may have grown up there once. Many early accounts of Prester John identify him as a descendant of one of the mysterious wise men from the East who, led by a mysterious star, brought gifts to Jesus in Bethlehem. Some identify them as Medes from a region on the east bank of the Tigris, others point out that the Chinese were probably the most advanced astronomers of the time. There is even archaeological evidence that a Christian people thrived in northern China until the eighth century.

Another fascinating clue is the story of St Thomas. Like Jesus's other apostles, Thomas travelled widely after the death of his master and, according to tradition, taught in India. The story goes that Thomas converted the son of a powerful Indian king and ordained him deacon. After Thomas's martyrdom the prince became leader of the Christian church in India and, when his father died, a powerful Christian king in his own right. Unless startling new archaeological or documentary evidence emerges it is unlikely that the true origins of the Prester John legend will ever be known. What the story does teach us is that a powerful belief, even if it is based on a complete untruth, can change the course of history.

Rasputin

• •

Mad, bad and dangerous to know

When they dragged his body from the frozen River Neva he had been dead for three days. He had been shot, stabbed, bludgeoned with an iron bar and finally drowned. Bloody fingernails indicated that even in the icy waters he'd had strength enough to try and claw his way to the surface. The empire held its breath. Many wept, many more rejoiced; Rasputin, friend of emperors and spiritual superman, was dead. Within a few short months the world was turned upside down by the Bolshevik revolution and Russia was never the same again. It was as if an age had died with the Mad Monk.

Few historical figures are more recognizable than the itinerant monk known as Rasputin. Tales of his huge sexual appetite, drinking bouts and irresistible hypnotic powers have ensured him a place among the great bogeymen of history. The "Mad Monk", as he was sometimes known, was undoubtedly a remarkable man, but it is puzzling how he has come to be so famous when the achievements of his life amounted to very little. For fourteen years Rasputin was a close and trusted adviser of the Russian empress, Alexandra. It was a period of desperate political confusion and disaster, events that Rasputin, for all his alleged wisdom, was powerless to stop. Rasputin has been credited as the secret mastermind of the revolution that swept the imperial family of Russia away in 1917. In fact he was a deeply traditional man steeped in the centuries' long tradition of the Russian church and largely in favour of the status quo.

Rasputin was born Gregory Efimovich in 1871. His birthplace, Pokrovskoe in western Siberia, was a typically traditional Russian village. His father was a successful peasant who ran a business carting goods all over the region. Life here was hard and unchanging. Russia's peasants had been freed from centuries of serfdom in 1861, but this made little practical difference to the yearly grind of survival in the region's harsh and unforgiving environment. People lived as they had for hundreds of years, praying for their crops at the local church, working in the fields and drinking to while away the hours of darkness. Young Gregory was no exception. There seemed to be nothing remarkable about the healthy, boisterous youth until a curious incident when he was twelve years old.

Lying in bed with a fever he had contracted while rescuing his brother from drowning in a frozen river, Gregory uttered his first prophecy. As visitors to the house were discussing the theft of a horse, Gregory suddenly rose from his bed and pointed an accusing finger at one of those present. The man was a respected figure in the village and hotly denied the accusation, but it was true. Neighbours found him later that night attempting to hide the stolen horse in the forest. Gregory gained something of a reputation in the village, but nothing more happened and the matter was soon forgotten. Certainly nobody suspected that the teenage Gregory was destined to become a holy man. He was known best as a tireless pursuer of women and a hard drinker. It was around this time that people began to call him Rasputin, which means "dissolute".

As Rasputin grew into a young man he began to help his father in his business and proved to be such a diligent worker that his father trusted him to make deliveries with the cart on his own. One day Rasputin had the job of driving a young theological student to a monastery at Verkhoture. The student was so impressed by the theological knowledge that his simple peasant driver showed along the way, that he extended an invitation to stay at the monastery and learn more. Rasputin accepted and remained for four months. It was here that the young libertine came into contact with members of a strange heretical sect known as the Khlysty. For 200 years the Orthodox church had been attempting to stamp out this resilient little group who believed in salvation through sin. The Khlysty argued that in order to reach holiness one must first pass through a state of sin. Their habit of holding orgies of sex and drunkenness made it an attractive idea to many. Although Rasputin always denied being a Khlysty member he certainly agreed with some of their core teachings.

Back home Rasputin, now twenty years old, married a local girl and settled down to raise children, but what he had seen and learned at the monastery would not leave him alone. One day he had a vision of the Virgin Mary as he ploughed the fields, and became convinced that God was calling him for a special purpose. He left his home and family and took to the roads. Rasputin walked over two thousand miles to the monastery at Mount Athos in Greece, and then back home again. He was gone for two years, and when he returned everybody was astonished by the change in his character. An air of mystery and profound religious power had drawn itself around him. He took to wailing and lamentation in the cellar of his farmhouse and blessed anyone who came to visit. Soon, the whole village was convinced that Rasputin, young tearaway and womanizer, had become a saint.

In 1903 Rasputin arrived in St Petersburg, the imperial capital. He had grown tired of the small challenges of his home, and had left his family again to wander the highways of the empire. His reputation preceded him and the uncouth wandering monk was received by some of the city's most important churchmen. Rasputin's mysterious air and apparent devotion won him the admiration and respect of many that he met. Like much of the rest of Europe, Russia was undergoing something of a spiritual crisis at the time. People were obsessively religious but found that the old ways of the church simply didn't fulfil their needs for a more direct, personal, religious experience. By 1905 Rasputin had been introduced to the imperial family, the Romanovs, and become a favourite at the court. The Empress Alexandra, a German who often felt isolated at the imperial palace, took a particular liking to this rough but gently spoken holy man from the wilds. The Emperor Nicholas was no less impressed when Rasputin cured his favourite dog of blindness.

In February of 1905 Russia had been rocked by the first stirrings of revolution. Strikes and protests that had looked like developing into a full-scale revolt were only quieted by the introduction of the empire's first democratic parliament, the Duma. The imperial family was badly out of touch with the people and saw Rasputin as a man of the people who could help to re-establish the old social order. Nicholas came to regard Rasputin as a friend and invaluable adviser. In truth the monk was just telling him what he wanted to hear. He disguised reassuring messages about the people's love for their emperor under the cover of the plain-talking opinions of a simple peasant. Nicholas confided his faith in Rasputin to a friend.

> *He is just a good, religious, simple-minded Russian. When in trouble or assailed by doubts, I like to have a talk with him, and invariably feel at peace with myself afterwards.*

It was not just Rasputin's far from simple-minded political diplomatic skill that placed him so close to the imperial family; above all it was his ability to heal the emperor's only son, Alexis.

Alexis was born in 1904, the fifth of the tsarina's children and the first boy. It was vital to the emperor that he should have an heir, the whole future of his family's dynasty, and the future of the monarchy itself, depended on it. The family's joy at the birth of an heir soon turned to despair when it was discovered that he had inherited haemophilia – a debilitating genetic condition that can cause a sufferer to bleed to death internally after receiving the smallest bruise. The disease had long been a curse hanging over the Romanov family and few who had suffered from it in the past had lived long. To many it seemed like the final sign that the family was doomed.

Where medicines and the best doctors in Europe failed, Rasputin triumphed. He seemed to be the only one who could draw the boy back from death when an injury threatened to end his life. In 1906, when Alexis was two years old, he fell over in the park and bruised his lower abdomen. For weeks he lay in bed tended by the best physicians the imperial family could find, but the internal bleeding grew worse and the child seemed ever closer to death. Finally Rasputin was sent for to pray for the boy. The holy man knelt by the sick bed for hours, then rose and turned to leave. As he passed the empress he reassured her: "Believe in the power of my prayer and your son will live." Within days the tsarevich was on the road to recovery. Alexandra's devotion to Rasputin became almost fanatical. She saw him as the only thing that stood between her son and death.

While Rasputin's reputation soared in the royal palace, it began to plummet in the city. Accusations of outrages against women and of generally wild and debauched behaviour dogged the holy man's every step. By 1909 the whole of St Petersburg society was in uproar over his behaviour. While some of the accusations against him were undoubtedly made up by those jealous of his closeness to the imperial family, a very large proportion were true. Rasputin used his position of influence with the tsar to get anything he wanted, including money, jewels and the favours of women. When he couldn't get what he wanted with persuasion, he took it. There was an endless stream of complaints to the emperor, but they fell on deaf ears. Influenced by the tsarina and Rasputin's impeccable behaviour at court, the tsar refused to believe that Rasputin was capable of committing such evil acts.

The emperor's refusal to punish or even investigate Rasputin drove an even greater wedge between him and the people. Now it wasn't just the peasants who were dissatisfied. Nobles and wealthy merchants increasingly despaired of the tsar's political short-sightedness. Meanwhile Rasputin was gaining power. His ability to influence the emperor's decisions allowed him to place his own friends in positions of power and to exile his more threatening enemies. The imperial family came to rely on their "Little Father" not just for personal matters but in almost every affair of state. Sometimes Rasputin's advice was sound and kept the tottering imperial throne in place, but usually he was acting for his own best interests rather than those of the empire.

In June of 1914 there was a stunning attempt on Rasputin's life. One of his many enemies in the church, a charismatic monk named Iliodor, hired a prostitute to walk up to the holy man in the street and plunge a knife into him. It would have been the end of any other man, but Rasputin was no ordinary man. His tremendous physical strength and will pulled him through. Rasputin survived but he had missed the most important political event of his life. At the same moment that the knife had been buried deep in his body, Archduke Ferdinand of Austria had been assassinated in Serbia – the event that plunged Europe into World War I. Rasputin had always been opposed to war, he knew how the peasants suffered, but at the moment that Nicholas was making the decision to commit Russia to war against Germany and Austria, he was not there to stop him. Within months Russia's hungry and ill-equipped armies had been devastated by the German military machine, and the coming revolution had taken its last step to the very door of the imperial palace.

In 1916 the power brokers of Russia's feeble and chaotic government faced a stark choice. Unless

Grigori Yefimovich Rasputin (1871–1916)

something was done quickly there would be an uprising that would make the disturbances of 1905 look like a picnic in the park. Either the emperor or Rasputin had to go. The government was dominated by nobles and aristocrats who knew that if the emperor was deposed, it was only a short step to the abolition of the monarchy and the end of their privileged lifestyles. Rasputin was the obvious choice as scapegoat. Not only was he reviled by the people but almost every branch of the establishment had a reason to wish him dead. Khvostov, a man who owed his position as chamberlain to Rasputin, hatched a plot to have the holy menace liquidated by the secret police. Such was the confusion and incompetence in the higher circles of government, however, that the police ended up reporting Khvostov's plot to the tsar.

The man who was eventually to free Russia from Rasputin's fevered grip was the most unlikely of figures. Prince Felix Yusopov, husband of the tsar's niece, was a boyish, effeminate character in his late twenties. His hatred of Rasputin was due in no small part to jealousy over his wife's adoration of the uncouth holy man. Yusopov was joined in his plot by Grand Duke Dimitri Pavlovich, a member of the Romanov family and therefore immune to ordinary law, a monarchist politician named Purish-kevich, a Dr Lazovert and a cavalry officer named Sukhotin.

On a freezing St Petersburg night in December of 1916 Rasputin was lured to a cellar room in Yusopov's palace. As bait he was promised a meeting with the legendary beauty Princess Irina. In the cellar Yusopov nervously offered his doomed guest a plate of cakes – each one had been laced with enough potassium cyanide to kill ten men. Rasputin ate two and asked the prince to play his guitar. For two hours, during which Rasputin drank a bottle of poisoned Madeira, the prince played song after song watching for any signs that the poison was taking effect. There were none.

Sweating with fear, the prince excused himself and went upstairs to consult his fellow conspirators. Purishkevich handed him a revolver and the prince returned to his guest. As Rasputin was examining a gold crucifix on the wall, Yusopov shot him in the back at close range.

The doctor pronounced Rasputin dead and the conspirators breathed a huge sigh of relief. Suddenly the dead man's eyes flicked open and he leapt on Yusopov with a murderous cry. The terrified men fled up the stairs hotly pursued by Rasputin on all fours. Purishkevich summoned up the courage to turn and face the ghost, he shot Rasputin twice more, once in the back and once in the head. Yusopov went into a frenzy of rage and laid about the body with a club until the snow was red and frothing. Rasputin was bundled into a curtain and dropped into the nearby River Neva. An autopsy showed that Rasputin had actually died by drowning – he was still alive when they dumped him in the water.

The conspirators were soon caught but, despite the tsarina's calls for their blood, they were given only light punishments. A few days later a chilling letter written by Rasputin and addressed to the tsar was found in the dead man's apartment. In the letter, Rasputin predicted that his own death was imminent and went on to say that if he was killed by the people the imperial family would be safe and rule for many years but, he warned, if he were killed by a noble then all the Romanovs would be murdered within two years. Slightly less than two years later the entire imperial family was gunned down by a Bolshevik firing squad at Ekaterinburg. Rasputin himself was buried after a secret service in the grounds of the imperial palace.

Inside the coffin the Tsarina Alexandra placed a final farewell letter to her beloved "little father".

> *My dear martyr, give me your blessing that it may follow me always on the sad and dreary path I have yet to follow here below. And remember us from on high in your holy prayers. Alexandra.*

The Shroud Man

....

Leonardo da Vinci's greatest achievement?

In 1898 Secondo Pia, an Italian pioneer of photography, took a photograph that revived one of the oldest and most hotly debated mysteries of the past millennium. Pia was the first to photograph the 4.3-metre strip of cloth known as the Turin Shroud – believed by many to be the cloth in which the body of Jesus was wrapped after his execution. Initially Pia had not been impressed by the relic, all he could see was a few dim discolourations and a very faint yellowish-brown shape that could have been seen as a man. When he developed his plates, however, he was startled to find that the negatives leapt out as a very clear image of a tall, bearded figure. In other words the image on the shroud was a negative; on Pia's plate it was the negative of a negative, therefore the picture was a clear positive image. In Pia's day photography was still in its infancy. The concept of negative and positive images had been known for less than fifty years. Who could have created a negative image on a strip of cloth hundreds of years before photography was even dreamed of?

In the climate of increasing hostility between the church and scientists throughout the nineteenth century, the Turin Shroud, like all other relics, had been dismissed by scientists as a laughable fake.

Suddenly here was evidence that, even if it was a fake, it was by no means laughable. Opinion was instantly divided. The faithful maintained that the image was of Christ himself and that it had been transferred to the cloth by some kind of ethereal flash gun effect, or a holy luminescence such as that exhibited by saints. The scientists set about trying to discover how the image, whatever its identity, could have got there, speculating that some medieval genius had discovered the principles of photography and used this knowledge to "create" a relic. From the earliest days of the enquiry there was one name that sprang to mind as the only one with the genius to perpetrate such a fraud: Leonardo da Vinci.

A number of scientists investigated every possible method they could think of to try and duplicate the shroud effect. The finest artists, using materials specially concocted to replicate exactly medieval pigments and fixatives, could not get anywhere near a match. At around the same time, a French pathologist named Dr Pierre Barbet carried out some shockingly gruesome experiments in pursuit of the truth about the shroud. Barbet noticed that the nail wounds on the image of the man on the shroud were through the wrists and not, as they were traditionally represented, through the palms of the hands.

Barbet used real human corpses to investigate the mechanics of crucifixion. First he nailed bodies up through the palms of the hands but it soon became clear that this couldn't have been how the Romans did it – the flesh simply tore and the corpse fell to the ground. Next, Barbet set about hammering spikes through the wrists of his uncomplaining test subjects and concluded that this must have been how it was

done. He also noticed that the wrist-piercing technique damaged a major nerve which caused the
thumb to retract in towards the palm. Both the
thumbs of the shroud man are withdrawn in the same
way.

In the light of Barbet's experiments it began to look
increasingly likely that the image on the shroud was of
a real man who had actually been crucified.
Bloodstains on the cloth also proved to be human but
nobody could be sure that these weren't a more
recent addition. As the decades passed and scientific
methods became increasingly sophisticated, every
test conducted on the shroud to prove that it was a
fake seemed, ironically, to strengthen the hypothesis
that it could be genuine.

For many years scientists yearned to have the
shroud material subjected to radiocarbon dating. By
measuring the decay of radioactive carbon 14 mole-
cules, this test can reveal with an accuracy of plus or
minus a hundred years how long ago a living thing
died – in this case the living thing being the cotton
plants used to make the fibres of the material. The
Catholic authorities had long refused these requests
because it meant the destruction of a piece of the
relic. Finally in the late 1980s the technique had
advanced to the point where only a tiny piece of the
material was needed and the authorities agreed to the
test. Three samples were tested by three different
laboratories along with a sample known to be of early
medieval origin – the scientists were not told which
was which. The results were a bombshell for the
believers. All three labs reported that the material had
been manufactured between 1260 and 1390.

As comforting as these results were for the scientists

Summary of shroud evidence before 1988

1. The Pollen

Forty-eight pollen grains were found during a microscopic analysis of the shroud. Most proved to have originated from plants found in France and northern Italy, but seven were from a kind only found in the Dead Sea region of Palestine.

2. The Fibres

Microscopic study of cotton fibres from the weave of the cloth revealed that they were from cotton plants grown in the Middle East. The method of weaving and bleaching the cotton was also consistent with Middle Eastern origin and archaic manufacture.

3. Medical Evidence

Bloodstains on the shroud were of human origin and their locations were consistent with bleeding from wounds received during crucifixion. Traces of a swollen abdomen is consistent with death by asphyxiation – the most likely result of crucifixion.

4. Circumstantial

General appearance and age of the victim corresponds to biblical and other sources. Hairstyle is consistent with that known to be favoured by Jewish males in the first century AD.

they did nothing to solve the mystery. The evidence now suggested that the image on the shroud was a photographic negative of a man who had died by crucifixion, and that it had been placed there in the early medieval period. The researchers were satisfied that they had proved the shroud to be a fake but were at a loss to explain how the fake had been created. Once again rumours that Leonardo da Vinci may have been involved came to the fore.

Legendary artist, visionary and scientist, Leonardo da Vinci was born in 1452. Ever since the "rediscovery" of his notebooks in the nineteenth century he has been regarded with awe. Da Vinci was interested in everything and his penetrating mind had insights centuries ahead of his time. Anatomy and the secrets of the human body were a particular fascination of his, and he is known to have spent many years studying bodies and body parts from the city's charnel houses. His sketchbooks contain startlingly accurate drawings of dissections and notes showing that he had an advanced understanding of how the things he was drawing worked. Among the notebooks are speculative drawings of fantastic war machines and even flying machines, as well as notes on all manner of natural and mechanical investigations. It's not impossible to imagine this great and voraciously inquisitive man stumbling across a primitive form of photography and using it to create something like the Turin Shroud. But why would Leonardo want to fake a relic?

Da Vinci's attitude to the Christian faith has always been a matter of conjecture. Unusually for an artist of his era, his most famous painting is a portrait: the *Mona Lisa*. But Leonardo also painted religious subjects. His *Last Supper* fresco is one of the world's most famous and admired religious images but on close examination it reveals some very strange features. Perhaps the oddest detail is the disembodied hand emerging from underneath the table and pointing a dagger at the chest of one of the disciples. Leonardo was meticulous in his observation of human posture and by no stretch of the imagination can the hand be interpreted as belonging to any of the other figures at the table. It seems to be an accusatory symbol, although exactly what Leonardo may have meant by it isn't known. The figure on the right-hand side of Jesus is traditionally interpreted as St John but, looked at with a fresh eye, it looks remarkably like a woman. Not only that but he/she is wearing clothes that exactly mirror Christ's. Another figure in the picture has his back turned on Jesus, a very odd pose in a period when the position of figures in religious imagery were invariably meant to convey adulation and attention to the Messiah.

It has been argued that the "woman" next to Christ is supposed to be Mary Magdalene, and that the figure with his back turned on the couple is a likeness of Leonardo himself. Evidence has emerged that da Vinci was a member of an ultra-secret sect known as the Priory of Zion – a centuries-old society dedicated to protecting the secret that Jesus and Mary were married and produced children. Whether this contro-versial hypothesis has any truth in it or not, there is compelling evidence from *The Last Supper* and other Leonardo paintings that his theological views were far from orthodox. Could the shroud be a part of his trail of clues?

In the 1990s two researchers who had become

fascinated with these bizarre images in Leonardo's works carried out a series of experiments in an attempt to replicate the shroud image. Lynne Pickett and Clive Prince became convinced that they had discovered how Leonardo could have done it. Using a very simple pinhole camera, essentially a box with a tiny hole in it, they projected an image on to a cotton sheet that had been soaked in photo-reactive chemicals. After several hours the sheet was washed to remove excess chemicals and then heated to fix the image. The result – an image apparently identical in appearance and make-up to the shroud image.

Pickett and Prince suggest that Leonardo simply acquired a body, as he often did for his anatomical research, subjected it to the rigours of crucifixion and then photographed the result to create the perfect forgery. Already convinced that the great painter was a heretic who despised the Catholic church, they see the fraud as a triumphant dig at the credulity and narrow-mindedness of his contemporaries. Obvious similarities between the face of the shroud man and self-portraits of da Vinci himself have also led to speculation that he projected his own face on to the image as a final touch of mischief – it has often been noted that the head of the shroud man appears slightly detached from his body. Could the Turin Shroud really be a snapshot of Leonardo da Vinci?

Many criticisms have been levelled at the Leonardo fraud explanation of the Turin Shroud, perhaps the most compelling being an inconsistency of dates. Leonardo was born in 1452, but radiocarbon analysis puts the date of the shroud around a hundred years before this. In addition, the first historical reference to the shroud comes from around 1200, 250 years before

Leonardo's birth. Both of these objections can be answered. The radiocarbon date could simply be wrong; although highly effective at placing very ancient objects in time, the method becomes more hit-and-miss when time periods are only a matter of a few hundred years. Alternatively, Leonardo may have used an ancient cloth to give the finished article a more authentic look. The second objection relies on confusing historical data.

The first reference to a relic that may have been the Turin Shroud comes from accounts of the sacking of Constantinople by Christian crusaders in 1204. This object, said to be a miraculous representation of Christ, was known as the Mandylion. The shroud at the Italian city of Turin that we know today may, or may not, be the same as the Mandylion. According to the story, the Constantinople shroud was taken to Besançon Cathedral in France where it remained until 1349 when it was nearly destroyed by fire. From there it was taken to the palace of the Dukes of Savoy where it again narrowly escaped the flames before arriving at its current home in 1578. Given the sketchy details of the story it's not difficult to believe that the original Constantinople relic may have been destroyed in either of the two fires and that the one that arrived in Turin in 1578, long after Leonardo's death, could have been a later copy. Even if the substitution was not deliberate the Constantinople Mandylion could have been the inspiration for Leonardo's work.

Leonardo da Vinci begins to look like a convincing suspect for the shroud fraud, but there are other possibilities. There is still the fibre and pollen evidence to consider that seem to show that the cloth at least was made in the Middle East in biblical times.

Many people remain convinced that the Turin Shroud is a genuine and holy relic bearing a true image of Jesus. Perhaps the truth is even stranger than the wild tale of forgery and photography in the fifteenth century.

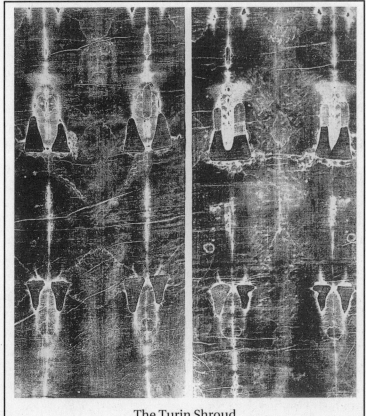

The Turin Shroud

Spring-Heeled Jack

●●●●●●●●●●●●●●●●●●●●●●●●●●●●●●●●

Nineteenth-century Batman

Few mysteries can match the case of Spring-heeled Jack for sheer oddness and wonderment. Over a period of nearly seventy years a bizarre and terrifying figure rampaged throughout England, carrying out a series of apparently purposeless attacks and outrages. The Victorian era, which gave rise to the maniac Jack, is a fascinating period in British history because it marks the transition into the modern world. New social structures, new industries and new and advanced scientific theories abounded in the period that began with the accession of Queen Victoria to the throne and ended with World War I.

Many cultural phenomena of the period are a fusion of the old and the new. Charles Darwin's theory of evolution exploded on to the scene during this period to be greeted as a brave new world vision by some and an unpardonable blasphemy by others. The Boer War was the first truly modern war, yet it was fought by a British army schooled in centuries of old-fashioned military pomp and ceremony. Sherlock Holmes, arguably the famous literary character of the era, is an intriguing mix of old world, privileged gentleman and modern philosopher grappling with the reality of evil in the world. Although less well known Spring-heeled Jack can be seen in the same light – a mixture of highwayman, sexual fiend and modern superman.

The first well-documented appearance of Spring-heeled Jack occurred in February 1838. Eighteen-year-old Lucy Scales and her younger sister were walking through the dark streets of London's Limehouse district on the way home from a family visit when they had a terrifying encounter. As they passed the entrance to Green Dragon Alley a black figure leapt from the shadows and towered menacingly over Lucy. Suddenly a blast of blue flame shot from his mouth directly into the terrified girl's face. She screamed and collapsed on the ground, her hands trying to shield the agony from her blinded eyes. Frozen to the spot, Lucy's sister saw the attacker turn and leap through the air to land on the roof of a nearby house. From there he disappeared into the night.

Rumours about a leaping madman who attacked women had already begun to circulate in London, but this was the first time that Jack had struck in the heart of the city itself. In September of the previous year, three girls walking on Barnes Common, Barnes was then a village outside the city, were confronted by a cloaked figure who tore at their clothes with clawed hands. In October Mary Stevens, a domestic servant walking across Clapham Common after visiting her parents in Battersea, met a very similar-sounding character. A man dressed in black descended on her from out of the shadows and kissed and embraced her roughly before bounding off into the darkness. She described the maniacal laugh and unearthly bulging eyes of her attacker – features that were to become familiar from subsequent sightings of Spring-heeled Jack. Two more attacks were also reported, both involving young girls and puzzling descriptions of a cloaked man who seemed able to bound effortlessly over brick walls, hedges and even trees. On one occasion strange footprints were found near the scene of an attack, they were very deep and seemed to indicate that they had been made by an individual who was either remarkably heavy, or who had landed from a great height.

Back in the city, two days after the attack on Lucy Scales, Jack struck again. Another eighteen-year-old, Jane Alsop, who lived with her family in Bearhind Lane in the district of Bow, answered the front door at about nine o'clock in the evening. A caped figure stood in the darkness outside. "I'm a policeman," he shouted. "Bring a light quick! We've caught Spring-heeled Jack in the lane!" Jane was back in a second with a candle, but when she held it up it was not a policeman she saw – the figure at the door was Jack himself. Immediately the leaping fiend blasted her with blue fire from his mouth and grabbed her lasciviously. Although temporarily blinded by the flame the plucky lass managed to land a punch on her attacker's nose and slipped out of his grasp. Enraged, Jack pursued her down the street, caught her by the hair and began ripping at her clothes again. Alerted by their sister's screams Jane's brother and sister came running out of the house, at which point Jack beat a hasty retreat with his bounding strides. Jane was badly cut about the face and neck by her assailant's claw-like hands and it took several days for her sight to recover.

Both Jane Alsop and the brother of Lucy Scales reported these attacks to the police and both gave very similar descriptions. The attacker had been dressed in black with a cape or cloak, and Jane described his outfit as tight-fitting and made of a material that felt like oilskin. On his head he wore some kind of a helmet and his hands were icy cold and had sharp claws. The most striking feature, however, was staring, orange-tinted eyes that seem to protrude from his head. A week after his visit to Jane Alsop's house Jack tried a similar trick on a house in Turner Street. This time the servant boy who answered the door grew suspicious and screamed for help before Jack could attack. His description tallied with those given by other victims, except that he noticed a large "W" embroidered on the front of Jack's costume. Again his method of escape was singular. The stunned servant watched as the mysterious visitor leapt over the two-storey houses that lined the street and disappeared into the night.

By now Spring-heeled Jack was known and feared all across the city. Londoners formed armed watch groups to patrol the streets at night, the police put out extra patrols and even the Duke of Wellington got involved. The seventy-year-old hero of the Battle of Waterloo strapped on his spurs, loaded a brace of pistols and took to patrolling the streets in search of the blackguard who assaulted defenceless young girls. Although there were endless reports and sightings of Jack most, if not all, of which were probably false alarms, nobody came close to catching the menace. Not until the 1890s, when Londoners lived in fear of another Jack, named The Ripper, was there such public fear and bewilderment in the city. Sightings began to crop up all over the country, but it wasn't until forty years later that the next convincing appearance took place.

One night in August of 1877 Private John Reagan was settling down for a long night of sentry duty outside the powder magazine of Aldershot North army base. As the night wore on he heard a strange noise on the road nearby. Cocking his rifle, the young soldier advanced nervously to investigate. He had gone no more than ten or fifteen metres down the road before he again heard a noise. Now seriously frightened, Reagan retraced his steps to his sentry box. Suddenly he felt an icy cold hand slap him across the cheek and he let out an involuntary scream. Another sentry came charging over, rifle at the ready, as Reagan reeled around looking for the intruder. As the second soldier arrived, a distinctive black-clad figure with a cape suddenly appeared and leapt high over the heads of the startled guards. Emboldened by the presence of his comrade, Reagan levelled his rifle at the intruder, who now stood calmly waiting for their next move, and shouted "Who goes there?" The figure grinned broadly and rushed towards the soldiers, both of whom fired wildly and without effect. A blast of blue fire dazzled Reagan as the cackling madman soared over his head into the darkness. Both sentries threw down their rifles and deserted their posts. Jack was back!

Almost immediately a bewildering number of reports flooded newspapers and police stations across the English Midlands. In a small village in Lincolnshire locals were stunned to find a cloaked figure leaping over houses and running at tremendous speed around the village. A number of people blasted the intruder with shotguns and reported that the shot seemed to bounce off him with a sound like stones hitting a coal scuttle. In 1879 a man driving his horse and cart home across a bridge over the Birmingham and Liverpool Junction Canal was assailed. Jack leapt on to the horse causing it to panic and gallop wildly off the road.

Reports that Jack had been captured, or at least nearly captured, were also not hard to come by. An army officer was arrested on a charge of impersonating Spring-heeled Jack in Aldershot, but later released; a young man was arrested in Warwickshire when he was found wearing a white sheet and trying to jump with a pair of boots that had carriage springs attached to the heels; in an unnamed Midlands town Jack had apparently been cornered by a mob but escaped by leaping over a three-metre hedge.

Sightings continued sporadically for the next thirty years. In 1904 Jack seems to have moved to Liverpool. He was first spotted in the south of the city where he was seen leaping from the roof of a water treatment plant. A few weeks later the caped caperer was seen scaling the steeple of St Xavier's church in Salisbury Street. As the gathered crowd watched dumbfounded, Jack leapt from the steeple and disappeared behind a row of houses. It was a fall that would have killed any ordinary man but no body was found. This stunt was perhaps Jack's last – almost seventy-five years since he had first appeared on Barnes Common Jack seemed to have finally tired of terrifying the nation.

Spring-heeled Jack is such a fascinating character that almost every retelling of his story comes with its own theory about who or what he was. A popular theory that has been in vogue since his earliest appearance in the 1830s identifies Jack with the Marquess of Waterford, an eccentric Irish nobleman and well-known prankster. The key to this theory is the embroidered "W" spotted on Jack's costume by the Turner Street servant boy, the aristocrat's well-known penchant for shocking practical jokes and his hatred of women. On the down side, the marquess had never been known to attack somebody physically, he was no more capable of leaping over a house than the next man and he died in 1859 – long before the Spring-heeled Jack reports died. It is Jack's apparently superhuman powers – the ability to make gravity-defying leaps and spit fire – that have led many to claim that he couldn't have been human.

Some writers have been convinced that he must have been a creature from another dimension or another planet whose physiology gave him apparently superhuman powers in our world. Against this there is the fact that none of the witnesses described him as anything other than a man, albeit a very strange one. But if Jack was a man, how can his remarkable longevity be explained? If the man who scaled the church in Liverpool was the same one who leapt out at Lucy Scales in Limehouse he must have been well into his nineties! It seems more likely that the original Jack was such an attractive figure that a host of later imitators carried on the tradition long after he had retired or returned to his own planet. But what made Jack so attractive?

The most puzzling question of the whole phenomenon is one of motive. What was Jack trying to do? He never killed or permanently harmed his victims, he never actually committed a rape and he seemed to delight in causing bewilderment and confusion more than pain and suffering. His startling costume, circus-like fire-breathing and occasional public stunts, in which he did no more than leap from building to building laughing, all seem to indicate a person obsessed with making a public impact. In everything he did, it almost seems as if he was mocking the values of Victorian society. Outrages against young ladies were considered the worst of crimes – witness the indignation of the bluff old Duke of Wellington. Humiliating the military by slapping sentries around the face and causing them to desert their posts was another blow directed at the heart of the establishment. Scaling the spire of a church would have been considered a shocking act of desecration. Even his general manner of leaping about and laughing was strictly contrary to the stiff-laced decorum of the age. Whatever else he may have been, Jack was the ultimate anarchist of his age, laughing in the face of everything the average Victorian held sacred. In many ways he can be seen as the prototype of the caped and masked superhero of the twentieth century. Like a kind of nineteenth-century anti-Batman he leapt in to cause mischief wherever there was stuffiness and decorum.

The Child of the River

. . . . .

Prodigious aquatic oddity

Sometime in 1958 or 1959 a year-old child was lost in the River Kuano which runs past the village of Baragdava in India's Uttar Pradesh region. The child's mother, Somni, was sure she would never see her son again – the River Kuano is swift and infested with crocodiles. Somni had a strange story to tell about how her son Ramchandra had been conceived. She claimed that she had been returning from mending a fence on the family's land during a heavy thunderstorm when a huge, menacing figure loomed up in front of her. The spirit, as she described the figure, threw her to the ground and ravished her – Ramchandra was the result. According to local legend a holy man had once dug a deep well near the village, and had been drowned when he climbed down into it to invoke the goddess of water. Somni believed that it was the spirit of this man who had impregnated her and that, a year after the boy's birth, he had claimed his son to live with him in the river. As compelling a story as this makes, Somni's tale was dismissed by villagers. Many suspected that she had deliberately drowned her child in shame at becoming pregnant by a man other than her husband. Then, fifteen years later, people began to see strange things down by the river.

One afternoon in February 1973 a local priest was

walking by the river when he caught sight of a strange human-like creature apparently walking on the water. As he drew closer he saw the creature, now clearly a human boy but with very dark green-black skin, dive into the water and emerge with a large fish which he proceeded to eat raw. The fish boy then lay in the water and was carried swiftly downstream by the current. The amazed priest told everyone what he had seen and when another villager caught sight of the river boy a few days later, people flocked to the banks in the hope of catching a glimpse. The aquatic child was nowhere to be seen however, and people soon lost interest.

Then six years later, in May 1979, Somni claimed that she had seen the river boy again. She said that she had caught sight of him asleep on the bank and crept up close enough to recognize a birthmark on his back that convinced her that he was her son. Villagers mounted a round-the-clock watch and the boy was eventually captured and taken to the village. He was described as slimly built with a distinctive, bullet-shaped head, feet as hard as rock and with incredibly dark, hairless skin that had a greenish tinge. The boy was unable to speak and may also have been deaf. He walked with an unnatural gait as if unused to being on land and had the odd habit of often holding his hand to his forehead. His character was said to be almost completely without humanity, he never gestured and had few facial expressions. Terrified by his captivity the boy made a frantic and successful escape attempt but, perhaps surprisingly, he did not leave the area altogether.

The river boy's experience of captivity had not been to his liking but the food he had been given certainly was. Gradually he began to accept food left on the banks by villagers, who made no further attempts to capture him and who came to believe that he really was Somni's lost son. After a time he grew unafraid of the people who came to watch him and carried on his strange aquatic lifestyle in full view of hundreds of witnesses. His main occupation was catching fish, but since he did this underwater nobody was sure how he managed it with such regularity. He would also eat spinach, leafy vegetables, raw meat and red chillies left for him by villagers. Many witnesses claimed that he could walk on water and remain submerged for far longer than a normal man. Details of the miraculous Kuano amphibian boy appeared in the newspaper *Probe India* and there can be no doubt that he actually existed.

Tales of the river boy's death reveal a tragic end to his remarkable story. One day in 1982 two policeman arrived in the village and, with the villagers' help, captured the boy. What brought about this sudden change of heart on behalf of the villagers who, up until then, had been happy to have the river boy roam freely, is not explained. It has been suggested that, having become unafraid of other people, the river boy began to act on sexual urges that drew him to the women of the village. Whatever the reason for his capture it was no more successful than the first attempt. Almost immediately he escaped and dived into the river. Later that day, towards nightfall, he was twelve miles away in Sanrigar. For some reason he made his way to a tea house where his sudden appearance so terrified one woman that she threw a pan of boiling water over him. Fatally wounded and in tremendous pain, the river boy made off in the direction of the water. His body was later found badly blistered and shredded by fish bites.

In his final agony, the boy who had spent his life in the river sought its refuge from the society that had first enticed him and then turned on him in disgust.

The villagers of Kuano were convinced that the river boy was Ramchandra, the son of Somni who had been washed away by the river as a year-old infant. Even if the river boy was not this child he had clearly been living in and around the river for most, if not all, of his life. How can a defenceless child have survived in such an inhospitable and unnatural environment? The river boy is by no means the only documented case of a child who has survived against seemingly impossible odds in the wild. Another well-known case from the same region is that of Ramu the wolf boy. Found in the forests of Uttar Pradesh in 1972, Ramu had apparently been raised by wolves. When discovered, he was about four years old. He had long matted hair, sharp uneven teeth and nails and walked only on all fours. He could not speak and never learned how to. His behaviour remained dangerously unpredictable throughout his short life. On occasions he would leap on chickens, rend them to pieces with his teeth and consume the raw flesh with relish. The wolf boy shunned people and craved the company of wild and domestic dogs – he had to be physically restrained from following wild jackals into the forest. Clearly his behaviour and character had been formed in a canine community. Why a human child should be accepted by wild animals rather than just consumed as an easy meal has never been explained, and there have been just too many well-documented cases to dismiss it as a myth.

Perhaps the most mystifying aspect of the river boy's survival is how he managed to avoid the river's numerous and aggressive crocodiles. Is it possible that in his case it was the crocodiles that accepted the child as one of their own? As incredibly unlikely as this sounds – crocodiles are not known for their maternal feelings – it seems to be the only explanation. Perhaps the river boy learned to imitate the crocodile's ability to stay submerged for long periods and to catch fish underwater by stealthy ambush. But why would a child stay in the water instead of crawling ashore at the first opportunity to seek shelter on dry land?

According to the theories of distinguished scientists Sir Alister Hardy and Elaine Morgan, water is a more natural environment for a young child than dry land. In her book *The Aquatic Ape* Elaine Morgan argues that humans spent a long period of their evolutionary development living exclusively in water. She argues that many features of present human physiology indicate adaptation to an aquatic lifestyle. One of her more telling points is the uncanny ability of very young children to swim with great ease – infants of other primate species avoid water and drown easily. The human child has a layer of fat that makes it naturally buoyant while other primates lack this. Human babies also have a no-breathe instinct that automatically closes the nose and mouth when the head is submerged, again this is not present in other primates, although it is found in aquatic mammals like whales and dolphins. Morgan has a wealth of other arguments that explain why the human skeleton is adapted to an upright position, why the female's breasts are positioned as they are, and why, uniquely among primates, humans have almost no body hair. Her case is convincing but perhaps the river boy example is still more compelling evidence that human beings were originally aquatic animals. Lost in the river at such a tender age, perhaps ancient instincts took over the child's development and reverted him to behaviour that served our ancestors millions of years ago before we abandoned the water for the land.

Monomaniacs

••

They just can't help themselves

We all have something of the obsessive in our characters: who as a child hasn't tried to count up to a thousand for no reason other than to do it, who hasn't had the urge to collect a complete set of something, whether it be football cards, the complete works of a favourite author or the postage stamps of tiny island republics? There is something in the human mind that finds sets of things compelling. Perhaps it is connected with our urge to find patterns in the world around us or perhaps it is a need for completeness, but whatever the explanation some people get it real bad.

Sir Francis Galton was one of the most brilliant British scientists of the nineteenth century. His contributions to branches of study as diverse as meteorology, mathematics and genetics have won him a permanent place among the heroes of modern scientific investigation. Part of the reason for his success was a strange obsession that dominated every aspect of his life. Galton was obsessed by the idea that every aspect of life and experience could be quantified and made to reveal hidden patterns. Galton, a cousin of the great Charles Darwin, was born in Birmingham in 1822. During the course of his long career he described the weather phenomenon known as the anticyclone, perfected a form of calculus and advocated the use of fingerprints as an infallible method of identification.

Among Galton's less successful projects, driven by his need to quantify, was a device that he claimed could produce complete anthropological statistics for any individual or group (whatever that could mean). To prove its effectiveness he compiled a "Beauty Map" of the British Isles, which purported to show the highest incidents of beauty and ugliness throughout the realm. After long experience of scientific lectures, both from the podium and the floor, he produced a boredom index which he claimed could precisely measure the degree of boredom or interest in any audience. It was based on the observation that attentive people sit still, with their heads in a fixed position, while bored people fidget and move their heads randomly from side to side. His index took a measure of the frequency of head bobbing among an audience and tied it to a scale of attentiveness. One of his more dangerous ideas came to him during a brief stay in hospital. Noticing the vast range of chemicals, potions and concoctions available to medical science, he resolved to try each and every one, in alphabetical order. Fortunately for his health he got no further than castor oil, the effects of which he found so disagreeable that he decided to curtail the experiment.

In October 1939 American World War I veteran Ernest Vincent Wright published *Gadsby*, his first and last novel and possibly one of the oddest books in existence. Wright was not particularly interested in the literary merits of his book, he wrote it to prove a point and his point was this: the most commonly used letter in the English language is not indispensable. Wright had achieved the incredible feat of writing a 267-page novel without once using the letter "e". A moment's consideration reveals just how difficult a task Wright had set for himself, words that were off limits include some of the most common in the language: "the", "he", "she", "they", "their", "we", "these", and "those", as well as the past tense of most common verbs that end in "ed". It has to be said that the finished work was less than a masterpiece, a fact that Wright freely conceded, and sounds more than a little odd:

> *Now, an approach to a girl's "Big Day" is not always just as that girl might wish. Small things bob up which at first look actually disastrous for a joyous occasion; and for Nancy and Frank just such a thing did bob up – for on May third a pouring rain and whistling winds put Branton Hill's spirits way, way low.*

Wright was by no means the first to attempt such a stunt, since the art of writing lipograms – works in which one or more letters are deliberately excluded – has a long history. The Greek poet Lasus of Hermione wrote his *Hymn to Demeter* in the sixth century BC without the letter "s", apparently because he couldn't abide its unpleasant hissing sound. It was a challenge that Wright obviously relished. In the introduction to *Gadsby* we get an insight into his rather unique character.

> *At first a whole army of little E's gathered around my desk, all eagerly expecting to be called upon. But gradually as they saw me writing on and on, without even noticing them, they grew uneasy; and, with excited whisperings amongst themselves,*

*began hopping up and riding on my pen, looking
down constantly for a chance to drop off into some
word.*

For most of the composition Wright used a typewriter
with the "e" key tied down. Amazingly *Gadsby* took
only five and a half months to write. Wright died on the
day it was published.

From letters to numbers. David Wimp, the self-
proclaimed Count of Riverton, Wyoming, has been
adding one to one for the past seventeen years. It all
began when a high school teacher offered a prize to the
student who could count to a million within nine
weeks. Adding with pencil and paper, Wimp only
managed to reach about 25,000 in the allotted period,
but his enthusiasm was only whetted by defeat. Many
years later, in 1982, after retiring from the army, Wimp
settled down with a calculator to make his first million
– one by one. After five years of fairly casual calculating
he reached his first six figures, every step recorded on
reel after reel of printer paper. It wasn't enough.
Gripped by his desire for more digits, he set about his
second million with zeal, taking only 436 days to reach
the magic figure.

Just for a change Wimp then switched to subtraction
and steadfastly denuded a million to zero in just 431
days of feverish calculating. By now he had created
more than forty miles of cash-till-style printout and
burned out more than a dozen electronic calculators.
Having limbered up, Wimp now felt that he was ready
to go for the big one. By 2007 he hopes to reach the
billion mark. Sometimes working five or six hours at
stretch hunched over his glowing calculator, the Count
of Riverton has settled into a rhythm of about 1000

calculations per hour, or a million every 1000 hours. Many people have speculated about Wimp's devotion, still more about the health of his mind. Wimp himself, more a man of numbers than words, says only "Everything doesn't have to have a reason, does it?"

Francis Trevelyan Buckland was a highly respected figure in the nineteenth century, a pillar of the British establishment. He founded the Buckland Museum of Economic Fish Culture and did much to improve the nation's salmon fisheries, but his life was driven by a dark and grotesque obsession; he wanted to eat at least one of every kind of animal. Buckland hid his disturbing ambition behind humanitarian motives. He claimed that the British nation was facing a food shortage that could only get worse, and that the only solution was to introduce new, edible, species of animal for farming. As the Messiah of this gourmet revolution, Buckland took on the onerous responsibility of tasting every kind of living thing he could lay his hands on. His devotion to duty was breathtaking.

At regular dinner parties designed to acclimatize the British palate to unusual new tastes, Buckland served up everything from rhinoceros pie and panther chops to slug soup and boiled dolphin head. When not at the table, and Buckland's table could be anywhere, he sought the company of rat catchers, taxidermists and big game hunters, all prospective suppliers to his twisted craving. Living in an age before home refrigeration, Buckland was forced to keep many of his future meals about his person or about his house in their living state. A house guest who made the mistake of venturing downstairs one night was inconvenienced by a hippo corpse in the hallway. On a railway journey a number of slugs that he had concealed in his overcoat for a snack escaped and crawled over other passengers. Buckland liked to travel in exotic parts, for him the whole world was a larder stocked with yet-to-be-tried delights. Although he relished mice on toast there were some things that Buckland simply couldn't stomach – more than once. He refused to believe that anybody could eat horse meat and doubted that mole and bluebottle stew would ever catch on. On his deathbed he was asked what he expected heaven to be like. "I think I shall meet a great many curious animals," was the ominous reply.

These are just a few of the people who have been compelled to carry out tasks that seem utterly pointless and meaningless to the rest of us. Others include Kea Tawana of Newark, New Jersey, who built a second Noah's ark out of scrap; Edward Leedskalnin who, single-handedly, carved a vast castle out of coral in Florida; or William Schmidt who spent thirty-two years driving a 2000-yard tunnel through a mountain peak using only hand tools and then never used it. As fascinating as the results of these mad obsessions may be, it is almost impossible to conceive of the amount of work that has gone into some of them, or of the kind of mind that thought them worth carrying out. Psychologists recognize a condition they name monomania in which the victim becomes obsessed with a single concern to the exclusion of everything else, but, as odd as these people are, they are not recognizably mentally ill. Often they have perfectly normal lives in every other respect. They recognize that what they are doing is odd, but have become so involved that they cease to worry about it – to give up becomes more peculiar than to carry on.

Forgotten Lives

•••••••••••••••••••••••••••••••

Who am I again?

Every year, tens of thousands of people disappear from their homes and families. Often there is no reason for the disappearance, no warning signs that indicate someone is about to go missing and no clues as to where they could have gone. At least some of these people are undoubtedly the victims of fatal accidents or even murders in which the body is never found, but this cannot be true of the vast majority – if it were, the police would be tripping over corpses in the street.

Sometimes the missing person is found or returns home of their own accord, but in many of these cases the missing have no idea of where they have been or why. Other people just "wake up" one day in a strange place surrounded by strange people without a clue as to how they got there. These are the extreme, and surprisingly common, cases of amnesia known as fugues. For reasons that nobody fully understands, individuals sometimes suffer a total collapse of personal identity that leads them to wander away from their homes and begin an entirely new existence. The stories of some of these fractured lives are among the most extraordinary tales of human experience.

One morning in March 1889 A. J. Brown woke up

feeling confused. He was in a strange bed in a strange apartment and he had no idea how he had got there. He knew he was a preacher and a God-fearing family man so there was little likelihood that it was down to drink. He got up, got dressed, had some breakfast and made his way down the street to a store where they sold stationery and sweets – he wasn't really sure why, but he felt compelled to go to the store as if it was an established habit. When he got there he was extremely surprised to find complete strangers wishing him a good morning as if he were a familiar face. In a flash his life came back to him. He was Ansel Bourne, resident of Greene, Rhode Island, which raised the question what was he doing as A. J. Brown outside a sweet shop in the town of Norristown, Pennsylvania, 200 miles away? Some people, who he had never seen before but who claimed to be his neighbours, came to Mr Brown-Bourne's aid. He insisted that they contact his family in Greene. His neighbours kept insisting that he was not Mr Bourne but Mr Brown, but they did as he requested to keep him quiet. Everybody was suitably astonished when word came back that their Mr Brown, sweet shop proprietor, regular churchgoer and resident of Norristown, Pennsylvania, for more than two months was in fact Mr Bourne, minister at Greene, Rhode Island, and desperately sought by his family.

Two months earlier, on 17 January, Mr Ansel Bourne had left his home early in the morning, gone into the town of Providence, where he withdrew $551 from his account, and promptly disappeared. A few days later Mr A. J. Brown arrived in Norristown and rented a confectionery and stationery store on the

main street. They were one and the same man.
Bourne's family in Rhode Island had been desperately
searching for him for two months when they received
the cable sent by Brown's neighbours in Norristown.
Everybody assumed that he had been murdered by
robbers after the large sum of money he was carrying.
Bourne returned home and took up his old life. He
had no memory of the day he had disappeared and
could offer no explanation as to why he had gone to
Pennsylvania. Three years later, Bourne was visited
by pioneering psychiatrist William James, who
persuaded him to undergo hypnosis in a bid to
explain his strange lapse. Once Bourne was under
hypnosis James managed to talk to Mr Brown and
asked him if he knew Mr Bourne. Brown confirmed
that he had heard of him but had "never met the
fellow".

Sometimes such cases do not have happy endings.
Luther Maynard Jones was a respected and wealthy
New York lawyer. In 1897, then aged sixty, Jones
decided to take a trip to Europe. He felt that he
needed a break from work and was keen to visit some
of Europe's great art galleries. Everybody expected
him back within a few months, but he did not come
back and every attempt to trace him failed. Twelve
years later a schoolfellow of Jones's was astounded to
see his old friend walking down a street in London.
He was even more astounded when Jones denied all
knowledge of ever having known him. He remembered absolutely nothing about New York or his life
as a lawyer and refused to accept invitations to return
there. Three years later he was traced again. Now an
extremely frail and poverty-stricken old man, he was
found living in a workhouse in south London. He still

denied any knowledge of anyone named Jones and insisted that his name was plain Luther Maynard. Just as friends were gathering money to bring him back to New York, by force if necessary, Luther suddenly died. His last words were reported to have been "Who am I then, please? Who?"

A similar case involved a famous New York eye specialist by the name of Dr William Horatio Bates. In August 1902 he disappeared from his plush home. His wife found it strange that he should have gone away without telling her, but soon received a letter from her husband saying that he had gone out of town for a while to carry out some operations that would bring in a lot of money. After six weeks without another word, however, she began to fear the worst. Suddenly, she received an anonymous letter which stated that her husband was studying medicine at Charing Cross hospital in London. She took the next ship to England and made straight for the hospital. Unfortunately the sight of his wife did nothing to revive Dr Bates's memory. Despite her pleading he refused to accept that he had ever even met her before. Heartbroken, Mrs Bates returned to New York and died three years later, never understanding what had caused her husband to change so drastically. Amazingly, in 1911, Dr Bates apparently fully recovered his memory and returned to New York where he again took up eye surgery. What he thought of his wife's death isn't recorded.

Sometimes cases of catastrophic amnesia strike people in the public eye. Colonel Raymond Robins was a leading figure in America's prohibition movement. The Volstead Act of 1919, which prohibited the manufacture and sale of intoxicating liquors, owed its existence in no small part to the wealth and political influence of Robins, who had made his fortune in the Klondike gold fields. On 3 September 1932, Robins had a meal with a friend and political ally at an up-market club in Manhattan. He left at around seven o'clock and vanished from the face of the earth. When he failed to attend a meeting with Herbert Hoover at the White House the following week, the president personally ordered a nationwide search. Many people feared that the colonel had been murdered by one of the many gangs that had sprung up along with the vast illegal trade in alcohol.

As the search got into full swing, a man calling himself Reynolds Rogers arrived at a small boarding house in the out-of-the-way mountain village of Balsam, North Carolina. He claimed to be a miner from Kentucky, prospecting for gold in the Carolina hills. The landlady thought this a little odd since gold had never been found in the area, but as the man seemed harmless and was willing to pay in advance she didn't let it worry her. After only two days, Mr Rogers decided to move to another boarding house when he heard that a man from Miami was staying in the same location. Over the next two months Mr Rogers became familiar in the area as he trekked into the hills every day to look for gold. He became friendly with a number of local farmers who would invite him round to partake of a little illegally distilled moonshine. During these visits he would often talk of having known presidents Roosevelt and Hoover, although he could never remember how he had come to meet them.

One day, a local boy saw a picture of Colonel Robins in a newspaper and recognized him as the eccentric miner, Reynolds Rogers. Within days the town was swarming with reporters, doctors and government officials. Robins was extremely bemused by this sudden interest in his life, but steadfastly refused to believe that he was Colonel Robins. Eventually the colonel's wife arrived and a tense scene ensued. At first Rogers completely failed to recognize her but gradually the truth seemed to dawn on him. Witnesses describe an agonizing conflict raging behind the old colonel's eyes until, suddenly, the light broke through and he rushed forward to embrace his wife, calling her by name.

Colonel Robins was able to go back to his comfortable life after only losing two months of his life. Others have been less lucky. Harry Miller woke up one morning in a prison cell with a bruised lump on his head. The last thing he remembered was leaving his home in Salt Lake City to enlist in the army, and being mugged on his way to report to his camp. His first concern was to find out if the police had caught the thieves who had stolen his wallet, although he was also a little curious about what he was doing in a prison cell himself. The guard outside his cell explained that he had been arrested after getting into a fight with a policeman who had tried to throw him off a train. The lump on his head had been the result of the tussle in which the policeman had found it necessary to apply some persuasive force with his truncheon.

Miller was a little confused about what he had been doing on a train, but then he remembered he was supposed to report for training and demanded that the guard let him go. Now it was the guard's turn to look confused. He gently pointed out to Miller that the war had been over for some time and showed him a newspaper to point out the date. Miller virtually collapsed on the spot: the last date he remembered was 1917, whereas the date on the newspaper said 1937. Somehow he had lost twenty years of his life. No one knows what became of Henry Miller; perhaps he too eventually found his way home.

As tragic as the story of Henry Miller is, it doesn't come close to the maddening torture suffered by a man known as Jerry Tarbot. He first became aware that he had lost his memory when he found himself in an insane asylum in California. All he could recall was serving on the western front during World War I, and medical evidence confirmed that he had been gassed and shot. Once out of the asylum, Tarbot, a name that had been given to him by a judge, tried to track down his true identity by visiting military hospitals and veterans' organizations. His case attracted media attention and a number of soldiers came forward saying that they remembered meeting him in the army. One identified him as a character known as the "grey ghost"' because of his uncanny ability to slip through enemy lines unnoticed. Unfortunately this ability to go unnoticed seems to have extended to his social life, because none of the soldiers who said they recognized him could remember his name.

Several months later Tarbot was in hospital in Washington, after trekking and hitch-hiking across the country on his continuing search for an identity. While in hospital he remembered once working for a company in New York that made surgical instruments. As soon as he had recovered his strength, he got on the first train to New York and located the building where he was sure he had worked before the war. Several staff in the factory confirmed that they remembered seeing him but, again, none of them could remember his name. The same thing happened to Tarbot time and again. He was recognized by a priest, another soldier and by more than fifty workers at a Goodyear tyre factory in Ohio. The few people who did put a name to his face were less than convincing. He was identified as French-Canadian George Beaupré, although he couldn't speak a word of French, as a James Talbot from Cuba, a country he had no recollection of, and as Bruce Harpin from Brooklyn. Eventually, exhausted by the appalling frustration of these dead-end leads, Jerry Tarbot gave up his search and disappeared back into obscurity.

The story of the man who loses his memory after a knock on the head, only to have it miraculously restored by another knock on the head, is a Hollywood comedy cliché. It wasn't so funny for Henry Miller, the man who woke up in a prison cell with twenty years of his life missing, but it seems to have been the blow he received when he was mugged in 1917 that short-circuited his brain, and the one he received from the policeman twenty years later that jogged it back into working order. In cases where no physical trauma has occurred it often seems as if some second personality, already fully formed in the mind of the victim, suddenly takes over. The Mr Brown who took over Mr Bourne's body was obviously still around three years later when William James contacted him through hypnosis. Colonel Robins's escapade sounds a lot like the fantasy of an overworked and stressed politician returning to the days of his youth, when he wandered the hills in search of gold. Luther Maynard Jones, the successful New York lawyer was also perhaps living out a hidden fantasy when he took off to Europe to pursue his interest in art.

Mental stress has often been blamed for these extraordinary episodes. When the pressures and boredoms of everyday life become too much, the mind just blows a fuse, effectively blanking out all responsibilities and cares. It is often asked how people who suffer from this kind of mental collapse manage to survive in the few weeks until their new identity is established. Apparently the new personality is able to block out the fact that it has no real past or memories. Sometimes, when faced with overwhelming evidence or close emotional ties, the block fails and the old life comes flooding back. Colonel Robins's wife described the conflict she saw in her husband's face as this struggle went on inside his mind. For some, the mystery remains too deep to fathom. The tragic case of Jerry Tarbot is an example. It is possible that Tarbot's original personality was so weak that it collapsed many times during the course of his life, before he found himself in an insane asylum. He may have actually lived all of the identities that people ascribed to him and he may have had a succession of weak personalities that people vaguely remembered but couldn't put a name to.

Based on his examination of Mr Bourne and other cases, William James developed his theory of the stream of consciousness. He pointed out that each one of us is only connected to our identity by a thin cord of memory. Every morning when we wake up we identify ourselves as the same person who went to bed the day before, but how can we be sure that this is the case? Perhaps sometimes when we wake up, we can be wrong.

Homo Eccentricus

● ●

Oddballs galore

Everybody does odd things sometimes, some people even make a habit of it but, for a few, oddness becomes a way of life. Although not strictly insane, these people's interests or way of life are so distinctive that they stand out from the humdrum mill of life like beacons. These are the world's treasured eccentrics. The word means off-centre, and that is just what these people are; wandering in the hinterlands of human experience, their eyes on goals that we cannot even see, much less understand. Eccentricity often accompanies brilliance, but it just as often accompanies pig-headed stubbornness.

Most eccentrics live out their bizarre lives unnoticed by the world at large. Occasionally the eccentric is wealthy or of high social standing, and then the results can be spectacular. For the people who meet them it can often be a distressing experience. There is an element of surrealism in the eccentric's behaviour that goes right to the heart of our sense of wonder and humour. Consider this description of an encounter with an eccentric: "At one social gathering, Ireland's chief justice reached for a handkerchief and discovered that the archbishop's foot had strayed into his pocket."

Sometimes it takes an eccentric to point out the error

of our ways – what looks like a kind of madness can turn out to be a revolution in thinking. One such Messiah of sanity was the distinctly odd Benjamin Lay. Born a Quaker in England in 1681, he was marked out from the beginning as an oddball mainly because of a cruel blow of fate that left him as a four and a half foot dwarf with a hunched and crooked back. He was apprenticed as a glove maker and then, aged twenty, decided to become a sailor. The deeply religious Lay relished the opportunity that his new career gave him to travel to the Holy Land, but he was so shocked by the behaviour of his shipmates that he decided the life wasn't for him. Back in England, Lay married and moved to London. His religious zealotry was constantly getting him into trouble and he was twice expelled from Quaker meetings for arguing in the hall.

In the early 1730s Lay and his wife emigrated to Barbados where he set himself up as a merchant. It was on this Caribbean paradise that Benjamin Lay first developed his lifelong aversion to the institution of slavery. The sugar plantations of Barbados were owned by wealthy Europeans, but they were worked almost entirely by slaves imported from west Africa. Lay was appalled at the treatment they received and railed at the evil of one man owning the life of another. Every Sunday he held sermons at his house which were attended by growing numbers of slaves. As well as telling them about the evils of slavery, a lesson they hardly needed to learn, he handed out food and Bibles. It was all too much for the plantation owners. Keeping a lid on the simmering unrest of the slaves was difficult enough without a cracked preacher stirring things up. Lay and his wife were soon compelled to leave the island and move to the American mainland.

Growing ever more contemptuous of a world that he saw as being full of evil and immorality, Lay moved into a tiny, isolated cottage near Philadelphia. The American colonies were already home to a large number of Quakers who had left England for a place where they could practise their religion without interference. These gentle and unassuming people were hardly prepared for the miniature firebrand who was about to land in their midst. In the middle of prayer meetings Lay would stand up and deliver a loud and violent harangue against slavery. On one occasion he burst a leather bladder filled with cranberry juice all over the congregation as an illustration of the cruelty and violence of the slave owner. As incredible as it may seem today, many members of this otherwise admirably moral and sensible community owned slaves. As so often happens, the mere fact that slavery was a widespread and accepted social institution blinded otherwise decent men and women to its inherent and very obvious evil.

Benjamin Lay was not blinded. Much to the embarrassment of his Quaker brethren he frequently sallied forth from his hermitage-like cottage to deliver blood-curdling denunciations of slavery. He refused to visit houses where slaves were employed and once even went so far as kidnapping a neighbour's six-year-old son to demonstrate to him how the parents of his slave housemaid must feel. Ten years later Lay's wife died, and he moved to a cave on a friend's farm where he whiled away the last years of his life reading and penning vitriolic letters to newspapers. In 1759 the eighty-year-old campaigner received the news he had been waiting for all his life. The rest of the Quaker movement had finally caught up with his "advanced" ideas and decided to expel all members who continued to own slaves. Benjamin Lay died a month later, a tired but happy man.

Japan rarely springs to mind as a nation of radical free thinkers. During the political and social upheavals of the fifteenth century, however, an extraordinary man appeared among the calm and contemplative ranks of the Zen Buddhists. Believed to have been the son of the emperor by one of his many liaisons with low-ranking ladies of the court, Ikkyu Sojun spent much of his early life hidden away in a monastery. There he received the best education available in his age and became fascinated with the precepts of Buddhism. According to the Zen monks who taught him, the only way to achieve peace and enlightenment was by rejecting the physical world as a dangerous and pain-filled illusion. These ideas impressed themselves deeply on young Ikkyu, but he saw things a little differently from his masters.

In those difficult and violent times many Buddhist institutions had become corrupt and lost sight of their own message. Monasteries grew wealthy from business, banking, pawnbroking and even brewing. The abbots of the important temples had become involved in politics and seemed to have abandoned the path of avoiding the traps of the physical world. It's a picture familiar from established religions the world over and the appearance of a man like Ikkyu was predictable. He saw plainly what many others could see, that the Buddhists had lost their way, but, unlike others, he also saw that he could do something about it. He took to staging shocking stunts to show up the hypocrisy of his masters. During a new year's eve party in the temple at which priests and monks were indulging in all the hedonistic pursuits that their teachings warned about, Ikkyu burst in waving a skull on the end of a bamboo pole. His message was clear; do not forget that we are all skulls beneath the skin and this world that seems so real will one day pass away.

Ikkyu took to the road to pursue his own vision of enlightenment. He left a letter for his abbot that read: "If you come another day and ask for me, try a fish shop, tavern or else a brothel." It was no joke. Ikkyu believed that the only way to escape the illusion of the world was by rejecting conventional logic and embracing both pleasure and pain. Where else should a priest be other than a tavern or a brothel? For many years he wandered the country scandalizing many with his outrageous behaviour and enchanting others with his honesty and humour. Everywhere he went he turned people's expectations on their heads and forced them to think about what Buddhism really meant. His pen and writing paper were his constant companions – until the day he died he wrote moving, funny and erotic poems that today are considered among the treasures of Japanese literature. It was not until Ikkyu was an old man that the institutions he had mocked all his life finally saw the truth. At the age of eighty-two he was invited to become abbot at the monastery he had left so many years before and was acknowledged and revered as one of the great Zen masters.

Not all eccentrics make a name for themselves the way Ikkyu Sojun and Benjamin Lay did. For some, their only purpose in life is to hide from their fellow man and avoid any kind of contact. In the case of the English aristocrat William Bentinck-Scott, fifth Duke of Portland, his enormous wealth allowed him to achieve

this to an incredible degree. As a young man the duke
led a normal and sociable life, even serving as a
member of parliament for a term. For some unknown
reason, when he inherited his title in 1854, then aged
fifty-nine, he suddenly became a hermit of the most
extreme variety. Ordinary recluses often have to resort
to caves or lonely cottages to satisfy their craving to be
hidden, but the duke was rich enough to create his own
underground world.

From two sparsely furnished rooms in a secluded
corner of his vast ancestral mansion, Welbeck Abbey in
Nottinghamshire, the duke issued instructions to his
army of servants and workers. Only his valet was
allowed to see and speak to the duke, all other
communication was conducted in writing via a pair of
letterboxes in the door to his chambers – one for
incoming messages and one for outgoing. All members
of staff were under strict instructions that if they
happened to see the duke around the estate they were
not to acknowledge his presence in any way. Even a
silent doffing of the cap could lead to instant dismissal.
The duke employed hundreds of men to create a
network of underground tunnels and chambers
beneath the old house. One of the first projects to be
completed was a tunnel, a mile and a quarter long,
from the house to the local railway station. On the rare
occasions when the duke had to travel into London he
would be driven in a curtained carriage along the
three-metre-high-tunnel to the station where the
carriage, with the duke still hidden inside, would be
lifted on to a specially prepared rail car for the journey.

For twenty years the army of labourers toiled away
beneath the ground. Fifteen miles of tunnel connected
a vast underground ballroom, large enough to hold

2000 people but never used in the duke's lifetime, a billiard room, a library and a huge subterranean stable filled with horses that nobody ever rode. The tunnels and chambers were lit by gas and spectacular skylights embellished with crystal. He also created an enormous skating rink for his household staff, which he insisted they used every day, whether they wanted to or not. In the last years of his life the duke only ever left the house under cover of darkness. On these midnight forays he would be accompanied only by a silent servant woman who walked fifteen metres in front of him carrying a lamp. The Duke of Portland died in 1874, aged seventy-nine. The splendid rooms he had constructed had never been visited by a single guest and the ballroom had never hosted a single dance.

Another reclusive builder was Sarah Winchester, heir to the vast Winchester rifle estate. When her husband died in 1881 Sarah inherited his twenty-million-dollar-share of the fortune, but she was not as pleased as might be expected. Sarah believed that her family was under a curse. A medium had told her that the ghosts of all those who had been killed by Winchester rifles were conspiring to wipe them out one by one and that she was next on the list. The medium gave the rather odd advice that the only way to escape the curse was to begin building a house, and never stop until the end of her natural life.

Sarah moved west and immediately began erecting what was to become one of the oddest constructions the world has ever seen. Beginning with the shell of an old two-storey farmhouse in San Jose, California, she embarked on a frenzy of mostly self-designed architecture. For thirty-eight years gangs of builders, designers and craftsmen toiled ceaselessly on the crazy mansion that was Sarah's only defence against vengeful spirits. When she died in 1922 the mansion had 750 rooms, covered five acres of ground and had cost at least five million dollars. Sarah herself had supervised the construction but she rarely went out and remained constantly hidden behind a thick veil. When she went into town to pick out materials, merchants were obliged to bring their wares out to Sarah's carriage and show them through the window.

As far as the actual design was concerned, the layout of the house was unconventional to say the least. Since she was more concerned with the objective of keeping the project constantly on the move than with the final result, Sarah's house evolved into a mind-bending labyrinth of dead ends, sealed rooms and stairs to nowhere – all executed by the finest craftsmen in the finest materials. An unfortunate guest who happened to wander off into the bowels of the house could be gone for weeks. Hundreds of doors opened on to other doors, precipitous drops or even blank walls. Many of the forty staircases went nowhere. When it looked like work was slowing down, Sarah would order whole sections of the house to be torn down and rebuilt to a totally different design. Dozens of rooms were lost for ever as they were bricked up to make way for new architectural lunacies. To Sarah's delight the top three floors of the house were destroyed in the great earthquake of 1906 and had to be completely rebuilt. The mania only ended when Sarah Winchester died in her sleep one night. The house stands to this day, a bizarre monument to one of history's great eccentrics.

In 1880 more than 10,000 people turned out for the funeral of Joshua Abraham Norton, the first and last emperor of the United States. Historians who point out that there has never been an emperor of the United States are among that species of literal-minded fools his imperial highness was compelled to deal with throughout his twenty-year reign of enlightened benevolence. Originally born in London in 1819, Joshua Norton arrived in San Francisco in November of 1849 just as the California gold rush was getting into full swing. By 1860 he had won and lost a fortune as a trader and issued a proclamation in a local newspaper.

> *At the peremptory request and desire of a large majority of citizens of these United States I, Joshua Norton, declare and proclaim myself Emperor of these United States.*

Few people noticed this earth-shattering political development in the constitution of their republic but Emperor Norton the First was not deterred. The populace soon began to notice their new ruler magnanimously walking among them attired in a second-hand officer's uniform and a tall beaver hat with a green feather. Even among the many colourful characters of his day, Norton stood out and his selfless devotion to duty won him the love and respect of his subjects. On his regular public walkabouts he would inspect street car timetables and construction sites to ensure that standards weren't slipping and occasionally, when the imperial coffers were a little empty, levy twenty-five cent taxes on local shop owners, most of whom happily paid up.

Everywhere he went the emperor was recognized and treated with the respect his majesty deserved. Trains and streetcars were free, meals were provided at his regular haunts and his uniform was replaced at the public's expense whenever it got a little threadbare. Determined to be a good ruler Norton carried out a number of improvements to his empire. Among his more dramatic moves was the abolition of Congress and the dissolution of the United States; both actions he regretted having to take but felt would benefit his people in the long run. When the Civil War broke out the emperor ordered Jefferson Davis and Abraham Lincoln to appear before him so that he could sort the whole silly mess out. When neither man showed up Norton was said to be offended but forgiving.

As great and regal as the power wielded by Emperor Norton I undoubtedly was, even he is eclipsed by the overwhelming majesty of Homer A. Tomlinson, Messiah and King of the World from 1952 to 1968. The teeming millions of the globe might be forgiven for not having noticed the reign of the greatest monarch the world has ever known, but it wasn't through lack of trying on Homer's part. Between 1955 and his death thirteen years later, Homer travelled to more than a hundred countries and carried out his public corona-tion ceremony in each one. His props were simple but charged with symbolic meaning. Homer himself wore billowing blue robes. The throne was a ten-dollar folding garden chair – convenient for carrying Homer explained – and the crown was a home-made affair painted gold. As he placed the crown on his own head in airports and public squares around the world, he held an inflatable plastic globe in his right hand – the symbol of his global dominion.

Homer received precious little thanks for his efforts to save the world. Although he claimed to have been instrumental in the Wright brothers' development of the aeroplane, to have ended droughts and epidemics and to have brought peace to the Middle East, the Russian government failed to notice when his coronation in Moscow's Red Square ushered in a new era of global peace and understanding. Craving at least a modicum of worldly power, Homer Tomlinson ran for the presidency of the United States three times between 1952 and 1964 – the gratitude of the nation was not forthcoming.

These are just a few of the world's great eccentrics. Sometimes they pass through this world unnoticed, sometimes they make great changes, but they always leave the world a little happier, a little weirder and never worse off.

The Lost

●●●●●●●●●●●●●●●●●●●●●●●●●●●●●●●●●●

Sometimes, it's best to hide

The instinct to hide from danger has been part of our make-up since the days when our most distant ancestors, the very first vole-like mammals, took refuge in dark burrows as Tyrannosaurus Rex thundered by. In modern times we rarely have to hide from giant lizards looking for a meal and only recreate the adrenaline rush in childhood games of hide-and-seek. Sometimes, however, the need to hide away for real does arise, or at least we may believe that it does, and the instinct takes over. For some people this has led to marathon periods of self-imposed isolation from the world.

In 1977 Mr D. B. Benson came home. His parents were more than a little surprised to see him, he had been missing since 1943. As an eighteen-year-old, Benson had been drafted into the US Army Air Corps. Never the sharpest tool in the box, he found military life and discipline hard going. After enduring a year of taunting and bullying at the Texas base where he was stationed, Benson decided he'd had enough and headed home. Back in Heavener, Oklahoma, a friend warned him that the military police would be after him for going AWOL and that he would be shot if they caught up with him. Benson lost no time, he packed a bundle of clothes, a pistol and some ammo and headed for the hills to hide out. He would remain there for the next thirty-four years.

As the years passed and the war came to an end Benson became increasingly adept at surviving in the wild. The pistol ammo soon ran out and he had to learn how to kill small game by throwing stones – his aim was said to be deadly, good enough to knock a small bird out of the air. His clothes soon turned to rags and he took to wearing any scrap of material he could find that had been left behind by the occasional backpacker. He also learned to catch fish with his bare hands. According to later interviews, Benson reported that he lived a happy, healthy and well-fed life. After several years he found and befriended a stray dog – which he named "Dog". The two became firm friends and a highly effective hunting team. When Dog died, the loneliness of his life began to get to Benson. His advancing age became another problem as he found minor injuries could keep him confined to his sick-cave for longer and longer periods. Finally, at the age of fifty-three, he decided to return home and face the music. He was granted a discharge from the army eighteen months later.

Another military man, Dmitri Kozlovsky, from the then Soviet Republic of the Ukraine, also spent more than thirty years of his life in hiding, although in his case it wasn't a healthy, happy outdoor existence. Soon after the German invasion of Russia in 1942 Dmitri, fighting in the ill-equipped and poorly trained Soviet Army, was captured and taken to a Nazi slave labour camp. Working as a bricklayer, Dmitri managed to survive where hundreds of thousands of his fellow prisoners perished. In 1944 he escaped from captivity and made his way home. The tide had turned against the Germans, and every available man was being thrust into the Red Army advances that were forcing the invaders ever further westward. Dmitri had had enough of the war, however, and had no wish to test his luck again. His family hid him in a concrete outbuilding with no windows and shut the door. He was to remain inside for the next thirty-six years.

In 1980, long after the last member of his family was dead, Dmitri was found by the police in the tomblike outhouse that had been his hideout for almost forty years. He was filthy, unshaven and severely malnourished. The solitude had severely affected his mind and he had apparently forgotten how to speak. His sorry state was described by the Soviet newspaper *Socialist Industry*:

> *He stood and trembled as if from fever and cried in a pitiful child's voice and tears poured from his colourless eyes eaten up by the darkness.*

Shortly afterwards he was put to work in a boiler factory.

An international airport is hardly the obvious place to hide, but that depends on what you are hiding from. Merhan Karimi Nasseri, also known as Alfred Merhan, has been hiding out in Terminal One of France's Charles de Gaulle airport since 1988. He is hiding from, or perhaps just defying, the bureaucratic indifference that has seen him shuttled from country to country for the past twenty years and cost him several prison sentences. On the "air side" of the terminal – the area before incoming passengers pass through immigration control – Merhan is essentially in a no man's land beyond the jurisdiction of any government. Given his experience of governments this suits him just fine.

Merhan's story is long and complicated. Born in 1950 in what was then a British-controlled sector of Iran, he was the son of a doctor working for the Anglo-Iranian oil company and British nurse, also working for the company. In 1972, after his father's death, Merhan went to England to study at the University of Bradford, where he stayed until his stepmother stopped funding him. When he returned to Iran he was almost immediately thrown in prison by the secret police for allegedly taking part in anti-government demonstrations. Four months later he was released and managed to get a special passport for emigration. Between 1977 and 1981 he wandered Europe searching for a country that would offer him asylum. Finally he was admitted to Belgium where he spent five years continuing his studies.

In 1986 Merhan managed to find out a bit more about his British mother – she was called Simone and lived in Glasgow. Merhan bought a ferry ticket and set off to find her. On the way he posted his temporary passport and Belgian residence permit back to the authorities, convinced that he wouldn't need them again. This proved to be a serious mistake. With absolutely no papers, he was turned away from Britain and sent back to Belgium, which also refused to admit him. He tried to get into France and was imprisoned for four months for illegal immigration. After his release he twice more attempted to get into the UK and was jailed for five months both times. Finally he moved into Charles de Gaulle airport in 1988 where he has been ever since.

Although the Belgian authorities promised to allow Merhan into their territory and even offered him money to help him get a life together, he has refused to budge. Having been rejected by family, country and the international community, he felt less than keen to trust his wellbeing to any one of them again. He spends his nights on a bench opposite Burger King and his days writing up his now voluminous journal or reading books from his library, which is stored in a stack of airport transit crates. Over the years he has become something of a celebrity and people often drop in to see him on the way into or out of France. He survives on donations given by airport staff and his occasional visitors. In many ways he is a twentieth-century version of the medieval hermit. Holed up in a no man's land he is a non-citizen sought out by the curious and persecuted by the authorities.

One of the strangest cases of a fairly recent hermit-like recluse is that of the Leather Man of nineteenth-century Connecticut. For thirty years, from the late 1850s onwards, the Leather Man could be seen doggedly pursuing a meandering route that took him on an endless 365-mile circuit once every thirty-four days. It isn't known exactly when the Leather Man began his extraordinary unchanging trek, since it probably took several years for the people who saw him along his route to realize that he was passing exactly the same spots on the same paths every thirty-four days. He gained his name from the bizarre and ungainly home-made suit that he wore, which was made of dozens of odd pieces of leather roughly sewn together. Clad in these strange, ill-fitting garments winter and summer he strode along the wooded pathways with a purpose that nobody could fathom. His punctuality was such that a curious citizen from the town of Forestville noted that over a two-year period the Leather Man's appearance in the town could be predicted to within two hours.

Despite his high visibility the Leather Man was as isolated from the world as any cave-dwelling hermit. He never acknowledged travellers on the road and was only heard to speak when he stopped off at one of the few houses he considered worthy of his patronage. For years he would turn up, regular as clockwork, at the door of a particular house in a town along his route and make his request for a little food or tobacco. Usually this was done with hand gestures, but at houses where he had been coming for many years he occasionally condescended to ask "Piece to eat?" The curiosity he aroused was almost unbearable for some people and many attempted to quiz him about his life, never with the slightest success. If questioned at a house where he stopped he would never return there. He would occasionally accept an invitation to down a few beers from townsfolk who hoped the alcohol would loosen his tongue, but he never said a word.

Any number of stories grew up around the mysterious Leather Man. He was said to be a madman, an escaped convict, the victim of a broken heart or even a witch condemned by God to walk his life away for his crimes. In 1888 he attracted the attention of the press when he ran away from a hospital in Hartford where he had been taken for an examination of a cancerous lip. One paper claimed to have solved the mystery and stated that the Leather Man's real name was Jules Bourglay, a Frenchman who had fled to the United States when he had lost the hand of the woman he loved as a result of ruining her father's business. The woman had been the daughter of a leather merchant who had promised her hand to Bourglay if he could make a success of the business. The story had no evidence to back it and was most likely the invention of one of the unscrupulous sensationalists who have always thrived in journalism. Whatever his origin the ultimate fate of the Leather Man is known: he died of cancer in 1889.

In many ways there was nothing extraordinary about the Leather Man; there has never been any shortage of lost souls wandering the highways of the world, asking for nothing but an occasional bit of food and their peace. What fires the imagination in this case is the fixed route and precise timing of the man's wanderings. Why would a man with no apparent ties choose to make the same circuit of an unremarkable area of Connecticut for thirty years? Given his total withdrawal from the world and human company, it seems plausible to suggest that he was the victim of some terrible shock or memory that drove him into a silent, friendless world. Perhaps somewhere within the area bounded by his never-ending circuit he saw something or experienced something that affected him so much that it became a kind of dark sun around which he orbited for the rest of his life. Some memory too difficult to face, but too powerful to escape, kept him circling for ever within its repellent gravity.

In 1978 Soviet geologists prospecting for iron ore in the remote Sayan Mountains of southern Siberia came across the hut of a family that had been lost to the world for forty years. Karp Osipovich Lykov was an Old Believer – one of a small and fiercely independent religious group who clung to values that had governed the Russian Empire before the time of Czar Peter the Great. Disgusted by what they saw as the decadence and heresy of "modern" Russia, they had survived in small bands on the fringes of society, settling in remote Siberian provinces and staying well out of the way of officialdom. Karp was the leader of one of the last of these bands when he led his followers deeper and deeper into the Siberian forests in the late 1930s. In about 1940 the band, now reduced to just Karp, his wife and his two daughters and two sons, settled in a rocky glade 200 miles from the nearest village.

For four decades the family saw no other people. They survived in a rough wooden shack despite winter temperatures of minus fifty degrees Fahrenheit, made their own clothes and boots and won everything else they needed from the land. Karp's wife died within ten years and the children grew up with absolutely no knowledge of the outside world beyond the dire warnings given to them by their father about its evils. When the geologists turned up at his door in 1978, a gravely disappointed Karp remarked only, "Well, come in, now that you're here." His daughters cried out, "This is for our sins; this is for our sins!" Karp, still obsessed by the politics of three centuries earlier, was not surprised to hear about World War II, the blame for which he laid squarely at the feet of ". . . that accursed Peter and his plotting with the Germans".

Whatever the rights and wrongs of keeping his children isolated from the world, when the world finally came to Karp's children it did them no good. Having grown up in total isolation, the four children, now all middle-aged, had no resistance to common infectious viruses. Within three years both sons and one daughter were dead. All refused medical treatment because their religion did not permit it. Karp and his one remaining child returned to the forest to live out the rest of their lives far from the evils they had feared for so long and that had cost them half their family.

Sleeper

●●●●●●●●●●●●●●●●●●●●●●●●●●●●●●●●●

The longest lie-ins in history

It's a well-known and often quoted fact that we spend at least a third of our lives asleep. Fortunately for most of us, we spread these years of unconsciousness across the whole of our lives in convenient chunks of about five to eight hours. Some people, however, are not so lucky. In 1876 a fourteen-year-old girl named Carolina Olsson from Mönsteras in Sweden fell asleep. She did not wake up again until thirty-two years later. During that period she did not move from her bed, speak or show any sign of waking. What could have caused such an incredibly extended period of sleep, and what effect must it have had on the unfortunate Carolina?

February of 1876 was fiercely cold in the small town of Mönsteras in Sweden's southern Smäland region. Near the town lived the Olssons – poor crofters with six children. One day, Carolina came home from school complaining of a headache and mentioned that she had fallen on the ice. Her parents thought little of it until Carolina became more and more listless and weak as the days passed. A few days later she was confined to bed and, that evening, she suddenly fell into a profound sleep from which she could not be woken. As time went on her parents grew frantic with worry, but they were very poor and hesitated to call a doctor. The days became weeks and Carolina naturally began to lose weight. Her mother fed her milk and sugared water with a spoon to keep her alive – the only food she was to take for the next thirty-two years.

Eventually the family felt they had no choice but to call a doctor – the first of many. The doctor, a local man from Mönsteras, examined Carolina and could only confirm what they already knew – she was in a trance or sleep from which she could not be woken. He tried shouting, shaking the sleeping girl and even sticking pins into her fingers but produced absolutely no reaction. Over the following months other doctors came to see Carolina, some more out of morbid curiosity rather than with any hope of helping her. Some described her condition as hysteria, others even dismissed her as a fraud or a "mentally backward person, pretending to be ill". The Olssons received little support from the local medical authorities and decided to take their daughter to a hospital in Oskarshamm. There the catalogue of medical negligence and disinterest reached new heights. Carolina was subjected to dangerously powerful electric shocks in an attempt to "cure" her. Eventually, when nothing worked, she was simply classified as incurable and sent home. After this time the Olssons received no official help or support.

As months and then years passed, the family settled into a routine as close to normality as they could manage. Carolina lay in the tiny two-room cottage tended by her mother twenty-four hours a day. Even those outside the village who had taken an initial interest forgot all about the tragic sleeping girl. Opinions in the village varied wildly from those who thought the girl's soul had been stolen by demons to those who thought she was just an evil hoaxer.

Eventually even the most disgusted or superstitious took it for granted. Life went on in the cottage year after year. Two of her brothers were drowned in an accident, her parents grew old and the family's fortunes waxed and waned within the tight boundaries of rural poverty. Carolina very slowly became paler and thinner, but life never entirely left her body. Perhaps even her mother gave up hope that the daughter she cared for so diligently would ever wake up. In 1904, after twenty-eight years of waiting, Carolina's mother died – she was never to see the miracle that was to take place just four years later.

On 3 April 1908, a widow from the village, who had been tending Carolina since her mother's death, entered the cottage as night fell. There was Carolina, wide awake and leaping around the room like a wild animal. She was shouting for her mother. It took a long time for Carolina to calm down, almost as if the energy of thirty-two years had been stored in her body and suddenly burst out. She was left weak, disorientated and very frightened. She had to accept the death of her mother and two of her brothers all at once. She also had to accept that the three old men who had come to see her were her father and other brothers. But, above all she had to accept that thirty-two years of her life had simply vanished.

News of the miraculous awakening swept through the village and then the whole country. People of all kinds rushed to gaze at the woman they were calling the Sleeping Beauty. The rush of attention can only have added to Carolina's terror, and yet she seems to have coped remarkably well. After satisfying a craving for pickled herring, she rapidly regained her strength. Within two months there was no sign of her remarkable ordeal. She had a healthy appetite, worked around the house and slept normally. A doctor who examined her shortly after she awoke described her condition as miraculous.

Carolina Olsson slept for thirty-two years and forty-two days. Chronologically she was forty-six years old when she woke up, but her prolonged sleep had apparently suspended her physical development. Witnesses describe her as looking like a woman in her mid-twenties and a doctor recorded that she had the body of a teenage girl. It was even reported that her hair and nails had not grown at all. The effects of her marathon sleep on her mind were apparently just as benign as they were on her body. A Stockholm psychiatrist who examined Carolina in 1910 described her as an intelligent, cheerful person who showed no sign of emotional trauma. He too noted her remarkably youthful appearance and commented that her teeth were very well preserved for a woman of her age. Not surprisingly Carolina could remember nothing of the past thirty-two years, but she could still read and write, and her memories of everything that had happened before she fell asleep remained unaffected.

Incredibly Carolina Olsson was able to resume a normal life within a very short time. The overwhelming interest in her story quickly waned when it became clear that nothing else was going to happen and Carolina lived out the rest of a long and healthy life in the little town where she had grown up. She died in 1950 at the grand age of eighty-four – few who knew her story were still alive by then and Carolina certainly never spoke of it. People who knew her in later life describe her as a hard-working, friendly and talkative person, who played a full and active part in the community. She only became silent and withdrawn when people tried to force her to talk about her lost years, many keen to hear the answer to the obvious question "what did you dream?"

To this day there has been no convincing medical explanation of Carolina Olsson's case. The most obvious candidate is a kind of coma induced by a blow to the head – Carolina complained of a headache before she fell asleep and said that she had slipped on ice. However, a coma of such duration has never been known to end with the victim recovering full consciousness and perfect health. Any injury able to generate such a long period of unconsciousness would surely have caused significant brain damage – something Carolina showed no sign of. It's true that long-term coma victims have recovered fully, but never one of such duration.

Hysteria, a kind of mental shock reaction, has also been suggested as a cause. Victims have been known to lose the power of speech, sight or hearing after suffering a fright or emotional trauma even though they have no physical injury. There are also cases of people who have lapsed into a state of trance-like sleep instead. Again, the extreme length of Carolina's sleep means that it does not fit the pattern of "hysterical" sleep. Also there is no indication that she suffered an emotional shock – unless it was something that remained suppressed in her mind even after she awoke. Many people at the time believed it was a hoax but it's almost impossible to see how this could have been achieved, let alone why. The Olssons incurred considerable expense trying to get Carolina treated and never attempted to cash in on the curiosity she aroused. If Carolina herself was the hoaxer it is simply not credible that she could have fooled her own family twenty-four hours a day for so many years – and what could have been her motive? She exhibited no indication of mental illness or mania that could have provided a motive before or after the event.

At the time there was no shortage of speculation that Carolina's sleep was supernatural. Deep, magical sleep plays a prominent part in the mythology and folklore of cultures all over the world. It is partly the mystery of sleep itself and its connection with the world of dreams that fuels these stories. Certainly the most famous example must be the fairy tale *Sleeping Beauty*, which is itself based on the Nordic myth of Brunhilda, who slept an enchanted sleep for centuries surrounded by a magical fire. The similarity between hypnotic trance and sleep has allowed magicians and witch doctors down the ages to persuade themselves and others that unconsciousness is the key to contact with the spirit world. For the rural folk of eighteenth-century Mönsteras the implications of Carolina's sleep were clear – her soul was in the spirit world unable to return to her body. In his old age Carolina's father claimed that he had seen her get out of bed three times during those three decades – once he had returned late at night to find her apparently still asleep but kneeling beside her bed in an attitude of prayer. At other times she was heard to moan or sob as if trapped in an endless nightmare pursued by demons. Could these have been signs of a battle for the soul of a young woman trapped between the sleeping and waking world? If they were, Carolina never spoke of such an ordeal and seemed remarkably unaffected by it.

Other Incredible Sleepers

Duration ... Who?   When?   What happened?

73 years
Bettina Pieri
1864–1952
Took to her bed as a fifteen-year-old girl and did not leave until her death aged eighty-eight. Did not sleep continuously but awoke briefly every three to four years when she carried out miraculous healings.

37 years
Elaine Esposito of Florida, USA
1941–1979
Failed to awake from an operation to remove her appendix. Died in her sleep.

29 years
Anne Shapiro of Florida, USA
1963–1992
Suffered a stroke and remained unconscious until awoken by chest pains.

20 years
Margaret Boyenval of Thenoles in France
1883–1903
Collapsed after extreme fright at a visit by the police. Awoke briefly in 1902 and complained of being pinched, then slept again. Died in her sleep 28 May 1903.

19 years
Gesine Meyer of Bremen in Germany
1884–1903
Fell into profound sleep for three months after an accident. After waking for the first time gradually took to sleeping for most of the day and eventually, in 1886, fell into a sleep that lasted until 1903. Awoken by fire alarm bells.

15 years
John Maceachin of Argyle in Scotland
1921–1936
After suffering a broken leg at the age of seventy-five, fell asleep in hospital and thereafter slept at least twenty-two hours a day until his death.

9 years
Mollie Fancher of Brooklyn, USA
1866–1875
Crippled and blinded by accidents at seventeen, spent nine years in a rigid coma during which time multiple personalities emerged that took over and "used" her body while she slept. Remained bedridden until her death thirty years later. Continued to suffer "possessions" by multiple personalities and was said to have supernatural powers.

8 years
Conley Holbrook of North Carolina, USA
1983–1991
Lost consciousness after being beaten by attackers. Named the culprits after returning to consciousness.

4 years
Unnamed French woman
1883–1887
Collapsed after an unspecified "'fright". Recovered after regaining consciousness.

2 years
Samuel Chilton of Tinsbury in England
1696–1698
Slept non-stop for three consecutive periods of four weeks, seventeen weeks and twenty weeks respectively. Thereafter returned to a normal life.

2 years
Elizabeth Perkins of Morley in England
1788–1790
Slept for eleven days, recovered for a week and then slept again until she died two years later.

Unlucky Lukes and Jinxed Jonahs

•••••••••••••••••••••••••••••••••••••

It just wasn't their day

When Roy C. Sulivan, a park ranger in Virginia, USA, was struck by lightning in 1942 he thought himself unbelievably lucky to have survived with only an injured toe. Little did he realize. Over the next forty years he was struck a further six times without fatal injury. Finally, in 1983, he shot himself. Some say he had been unlucky in love, others that he was just tired of waiting.

Luck, good or bad, is perhaps the most universally recognized paranormal phenomenon. Everybody knows a lucky individual, someone who seems to constantly win raffles or lotteries, and everybody has experienced a day when their luck has run low, when every little thing seems to fall within that narrow range of possibility that makes it inconvenient or troublesome. When we experience good luck we call it fortune, but when the luck is bad we call it fate or a jinx. We all experience a little of both in our lives but for some individuals it almost seems as if they are being targeted by some malign intelligence. This figure is often referred to as the Cosmic Joker, although his pranks are invariably more amusing to the bystander than to his victim.

In 1994 Dominique Guiholt seemed to have the god of luck smiling on her when she miraculously survived a 3700-foot fall after her parachute failed to open. Landing on bales of hay in a field, the stunned Guiholt was able to walk away from her death plummet completely unharmed. Four hours later she slipped on her bathroom floor, cracked her head on the toilet bowl and died instantly. This is just one of many cases in which some kind of balance of luck seems to come into play, what the Cosmic Joker gives with one hand he takes with the other.

Roads are apparently a favoured location for this form of double jeopardy. In 1993 Charles Millbank survived a potentially lethal collision with a roadside electricity pole in Essex. His car careered off the road and came to rest in a ditch. Happy to be alive, Charles hopped out and scrambled up the bank, where he inadvertently grabbed the 11,000-volt cable that the collision had brought down and was instantly fried. Woodrow Creekmore had a similar encounter when his car skidded on an icy road and slammed into a telegraph pole in Oklahoma. Creekmore climbed out of his mangled car uninjured, but as he stood by the roadside hoping to hitch a lift, the telegraph pole he had hit slowly keeled over and struck him fatally on the head.

Sometimes the Cosmic Joker is not satisfied with one victim and pulls the same trick again and again to create a bizarre chain of deaths. Yooket Paen died when she slipped and fell in the mud on her farm near Bangkok, Thailand. It wasn't the fall that killed her however; as she went over she made a grab for a cable that turned out to be live and she was electrocuted. Later that day her sister, Yooket Pan, was explaining the accident to her neighbour when she slipped and fell and, almost inevitably, grabbed the same cable and was also killed. While some death chains, such as the one that saw six members of the Smenghi family drowned in a factory water intake pipe as they tried to rescue each other, need no more than a faulty appliance or a freakishly dangerous stretch of water to work their magic, others seem to be carried around by an individual who becomes a curse to whoever he meets. On such unfortunate individual was an Hungarian artist named Hans Kinnow.

In the late 1930s Kinnow had just finished a commissioned portrait when his subject, a millionaire's wife, keeled over with heart failure. When his next sitter died within a few days of his portrait being finished, and then the one after that died too, Kinnow vowed to give up painting. A few years later the artist fell in love and decided to get married; forgetting his earlier vow, he agreed to paint his fiancée – she was dead from pneumonia within a week. Kinnow was a broken man, he gave up painting entirely and became a poverty-stricken odd-job man. When he died in 1938 the landlady at his cheap lodging house found a crayon sketch dated the previous day beside his bed; it was a self-portrait.

A similarly inexplicable chain of coincidental deaths is connected to another Hungarian, a composer named Reszo Serress. One day in December 1932 Seress, then living in Paris, was having a particularly bad day. His music career was going nowhere, he had no money and his girlfriend had just left him. Immersed in his miseries he sat at his piano and idly began improvising a gloomy tune. Amazingly the fruit of his afternoon's work turned out to be his first success. The tune, called *Gloomy Sunday*, was accepted by a publisher and distributed in sheet music form all over the world.

Seress was thrilled, but his happiness was short-lived. A spate of apparent suicides began to be connected with his creation. A young man who had requested a band in Berlin to play the tune later blew his brains out with a revolver; a copy of the sheet music was found by the body of a young shop assistant who hanged herself in the same city; a young woman who gassed herself in New York requested that *Gloomy Sunday* be played at her funeral; and a woman in north London was found dead from an overdose of barbiturates when neighbours broke into her house to find out why her record player was repeating the same song over and over; the song – *Gloomy Sunday*.

When chain deaths affect the same family or group of people there is talk of jinxes or curses. America's Kennedy clan is perhaps the most famous example of a bad-luck family. Even before the assassinations of John and Robert Kennedy the family had suffered a string of fatal tragedies. The plane crash that killed John Kennedy's son in 1999 is just the latest in a tragic chain. The Ruckenstahl family of the small village of Mitteraich in Austria may not be as famous as the Kennedys but their weight of tragedy is just as unbelievable. In 1975, nineteen-year-old Peter Ruckenstahl was killed by a car at a spot where the main road through the village runs by the railway. Six months later, his brother Joseph Jnr was hit and killed by a train near the same spot as he tried to cross the tracks on a moped. In 1979 Joseph and Peter's father was killed by a train at the same spot. A tombstone-shaped kilometre marker near the fatal junction summed up the irony for distraught Aloisia, wife of Joseph and mother of Peter and Joseph Jnr. Less than a year later her last surviving son, Walter, ran into a lamp-post on his sledge, ruptured his spleen and later died in hospital.

Coincidences are a common source of wonder and amazement. The deadly hand of the Cosmic Joker seems to take particular delight in marking the cards of fate with these inexplicable events. Shortly after a performance as the lead in the Puccini opera *Tosca*, in which the heroine plummets to her death from the walls of a castle in the final scene, singer Marie Collier was meeting her financial agent at her London home. Collier had got the role when the original star, the legendary Maria Callas, had pulled out at the last minute, and the excellent critical reception her performances had won looked set to put her on the road to international stardom. Unfortunately, during a conversation with her agent, she opened a balcony window, stepped out and plummeted thirty feet to her death on the street below.

Sue Alton of Surrey in England met a similarly coincidental death when her horse bolted and threw her, head first, into a stone monument by the side of the bridleway. The monument had been erected to commemorate the death of Samuel Wilberforce, Bishop of Winchester, killed on that spot in 1837 when his horse stumbled and threw him on his head. When Erskine Ebbin of Hamilton in Canada was knocked from his moped by a taxi and killed in 1975, it was an unbelievable blow for his family. On the same day of the previous year Erskine's brother Neville had also been knocked from his moped and killed. Both brothers were seventeen when they died, both were killed on the same stretch of road and the taxi involved in both accidents was being driven by the same driver and carrying the same passenger on both occasions.

Given the ever-present danger of death by coincidence it seems that some people are just asking for trouble. In 1987 Kobus Slabbert was lecturing children on the dangers of the crocodile-infested Zambesi river. Standing on the bank of the river at a school picnic, Slabbert was warning children to stay out of the water when a giant croc grabbed him by the leg, dragged him under and ate him. In December of 1980 a TV film crew watched in horror as five mountain rescue policemen, who had agreed to help film a documentary about the dangers of avalanches in the French Alps, were swept to their deaths by a huge avalanche. Mike Stewert, president of the Auto Convoy Company, was making a safety film about the dangers of low-level suburban bridges when the flatbed truck he was standing on passed under a particularly good example, killing him instantly. The ghost of the unnamed party guest who fell into a swimming pool fully clothed and drowned, must have cursed the day he accepted an invitation to a lifeguard celebration in New Orleans to mark a whole year without a single recorded death.

Bad luck isn't always fatal, in fact sometimes it can be just the opposite. Peter Ditert, a lonely man suffering from depression, was plagued by a particularly perverse form of bad luck. He started his marathon saga of attempted suicide by leaping in front of a speeding car, which resulted in nothing worse than concussion. Next he tried electrocution by plunging a hair dryer into his bath, but the fuse blew. Then he slashed his wrists and took rat poison, but neither did the trick. An attempt to blow himself up by filling his house with gas came to nothing as did driving off an embankment at seventy miles per hour. The home-made pistol he had made to shoot himself with jammed, and the brake fluid he drank just made him vomit. Finally he drove down a crowded street at breakneck speed deliberately ramming fourteen other cars; he suffered only a headache. Suicidal Spaniard Abel Ruiz was similarly disappointed when close encounters with a speeding express train and a truck failed to result in anything more than cuts and bruises. As he left the hospital he promised doctors that he would not try to take his own life again, but a few hours later he was back. He had almost been trampled to death by a stampeding horse; this time a complete accident.

Examples of unlucky days that beggar belief are not hard to find. Shortly before his wedding in 1994 Paul McLean checked up on the arrangements he had made for the big day. The first nasty surprise came when he discovered that the church had collapsed. When he tried to contact the priest who was supposed to perform the ceremony, McLean found that he had suffered a nervous breakdown. Further enquiries revealed that the Los Angeles reception venue had burned down and that his new home had neither electricity nor water.

Of all the dubious japes and terminal tricks played by the Cosmic Joker, coincidence is clearly a favourite. A classic example is the case of an armed robber serving an eight-year sentence in Argentina. With time on his hands, the man decided to try and trace the father he had never met and hired a private detective for the job. After several months the detective found the inmate's father – he was the warder at the prison where he was serving his sentence. Another attack of coincidence struck newsagent Dennis Brightly of Suffolk. Seconds after pinning a "No Milk Today" sign outside his shop, a float carrying over a thousand pints of the stuff swerved to avoid a car and smashed through his front window.

A notorious example of coincidence connects the deaths of two of the United States's most popular presidents. Both John F. Kennedy and Abraham Lincoln were assassinated at the height of their popularity; Lincoln in 1865 and Kennedy in 1963. The endless research that has gone into the lives of both men has turned up a series of remarkable coincidences that link the similar deaths of these two men on some mysterious level.

Many people have been tempted to conclude that coincidence and strange luck point to the existence of a power, perhaps mischievous and perhaps beneficent, that is directing our lives, but it is important to put the phenomenon in perspective. Coincidence can be defined as the unexpected concurrence of events not causally connected – in other words when two things that seem to be connected happen together but where one does not, or could not, obviously cause the other. The power of coincidence to attract our wonder lies in the very fact that two unrelated events seem to be connected. For example, if the truck that had crashed into Dennis Brightly's newsagents had been carrying bread rather than milk, then there is no coincidence and no interest.

Coincidence rests entirely on the significance we place on events. Every event that happens in our lives is effectively a million-to-one shot. The fact that it is five to eleven as I write this and the fact that I am

Coincidences in the lives and deaths of Kennedy and Lincoln

1. Lincoln was elected president in 1860, Kennedy exactly a century later in 1960.

2. The killers, John Wilkes Booth and Lee Harvey Oswald, were born in 1839 and 1939 respectively.

3. Both men were shot from behind in the head, both men were killed in the presence of their wives.

4. Both assassins were killed before coming to trial.

5. Lincoln was shot in Ford's Theatre, Kennedy in a Ford car.

6. The successors of both presidents were named Johnson and were Democrats from the south.

7. Booth shot Lincoln in a theatre and escaped to a warehouse; Oswald shot Kennedy from a warehouse and escaped to a theatre.

8. Lincoln's secretary, whose first name was John, warned him not to go to the theatre. Kennedy's secretary, whose name was Lincoln, advised him not to go to Dallas.

9. Both presidents suffered the loss of a son while they were in the White House.

10. Andrew Johnson was born in 1808; Lyndon Johnson in 1908.

11. The names Lincoln and Kennedy each contain seven letters. The names John Wilkes Booth and Lee Harvey Oswald each contain fifteen letters. The names Andrew Johnson and Lyndon Johnson each contain thirteen letters.

wearing blue socks are completely coincidental – but they are not considered significant. If you walk down a busy city street you will pass hundreds of people and the chances that you would have passed any one of those people in that particular place at that particular time are extremely small – but, unless one of them turns out to be your long-lost brother, you will attribute absolutely no significance to any of those million-to-one chance encounters.

On the other hand, day-to-day experience teaches us that sometimes things happen which cannot be explained away by talk of chance and probability. Sometimes it seems frighteningly possible that the Cosmic Joker has us all in the palm of his hand. The demise of Italian Salvatore Chirilino is food for thought: walking along a clifftop in Vibo Marina, he slipped on wet grass and fell 150 feet to his death. Why was he so close to the edge? He was trying to pick a lucky four-leaf clover.

Here Be Cannibals

●●●●●●●●●●●●●●●●●●●●●●●●●●●●●●●●●●

A taste for long-pig

The history of cannibalism is a long and fascinating one full of incidents of horror, desperation and, above all, bewildering contradiction. The act of eating another human being is widely regarded as the most repugnant of sins, and yet it is far more common than might be expected. Many people have been cannibals for many different reasons. Among certain tribes cannibalism has been performed as a kind of ancestor worship; in situations of extreme deprivation it has been resorted to as a measure of desperation; in the dark world of the psychopath, cannibalism has turned up time and again as a part of the killer's ritual of death and empowerment.

Among big-brained mammals, the so-called "higher animals", true cannibalism is very rare. The chimpanzee, our closest living relative in the animal kingdom, is the one animal known to practise it on a regular basis. The behaviour of wild chimpanzee troupes offers a fascinating insight into the origins of many human patterns of behaviour. Chimpanzee groups live in strictly defined territories that are defended and maintained by regular patrols. Sometimes, when patrols from rival troupes meet on the border of their respective territories, vicious battles break out. An individual unfortunate enough to be captured by the other side will almost certainly be beaten to death, and is likely to be torn apart and consumed in an orgy of violent gluttony. Perhaps this is a clue to the origins of our feelings about cannibalism. The pure animal violence of tearing an enemy limb from limb and eating the flesh is an idea that the modern mind shies away from, yet it is an idea that our animal brains cannot help but find exciting and powerful. Whatever the source of our feelings about it, cannibalism crops up in some very unexpected places and gives rise to some surprising reactions.

In 1990 a horrifying tale came to the attention of the world. Wang Guang, owner of the White Temple restaurant in China's Hainan province, had been making a tidy profit from selling his popular Sichuan-style dumplings. They were cheap and spicily tasty and Wang often sold out. It wasn't until the parents of a young woman who had been killed in a car crash made an apparently unconnected gruesome discovery, that Wang's little scam came to light. The grieving relatives had unexpectedly returned to the crematorium to say a last farewell to their daughter when it was discovered that the flesh of her thighs and buttocks had been hacked off. During the course of the investigation the culprit was identified as a worker at the crematorium named Hui who turned out to be the brother of Wang Guang. For at least three years Hui had been supplying his brother with free, fresh meat – hacked directly from corpses delivered to the crematorium.

Another case of Chinese food that you probably wouldn't want to take away was uncovered on the holiday island of Coloane, part of the Portuguese colony of Macao. In June 1985 a family of nine suddenly disappeared from the restaurant they owned at the Black Sands tourist resort. The search for the Cheng family, including their five children and a servant, revealed nothing until a dozen severed limbs were found washed up on the resort's beach. Police decided to investigate the new owner of the Chengs' restaurant, Wong Chi Hang. It emerged that Wong and Cheng Lam, the head of the Cheng family, had been involved in a long-running feud over gambling debts. Wong had poisoned the adults of the family and strangled the children. He then simply took over the family's business and home. After cutting up the bodies he had disposed of parts in the sea and the rest he had used to make dim sum for customers at the restaurant. Wong had even boiled the skulls of his victims to make the soup.

In cases of blatant and perverse criminality such as these, society finds it easy to maintain its moral indignation. In cases where survival is at stake, however, public reaction is not so clear cut. In 1884 a fifteen-metre yacht named the *Mignonette* was on its way to new owners in Australia, when it ran into extreme weather off the coast of Africa and sank in the South Atlantic. The four-man crew all managed to escape in the vessel's sloop but had no drinking water or food. After fifteen days of scorching heat and freezing nights, tossed about on the shark-infested waters, all four men were close to death. One of them, a youth named Richard Parker who was not yet eighteen, was in a worse state than any. He had drunk sea water and was also suffering from diarrhoea. The other three discussed drawing lots to decide who should be sacrificed, but the choice was obvious. As Parker lay delirious in the bottom of the boat Captain Tom Dudley slit his throat and the three collected his blood as he died and drank it. The boy's heart and liver were removed and eaten immediately. Strips of flesh were then cut from the body and the rest of the corpse slung overboard.

Nine days later the three surviving crewmen of the *Mignonette* were picked up by a German trading ship, the *Montezuma*. Dudley compiled a full and frank account of the fate of his ship and his crew mate Richard Parker during the journey back to England. All three men were arrested as soon as the *Montezuma* docked. Parker's family received his pay and the three prisoners were generally regarded as heroes rather than fiends. Despite press stories filled with sympathy for the men, the government had little choice but to charge them with murder. The trial was held in Exeter and later relocated to London. It attracted enormous public attention and endless articles exonerating the crew for their actions. The adulation that the *Mignonette* three received from some quarters was quite incredible considering the generally accepted views of the time. This was the height of the British Empire and cannibalism was regarded as a barbarous custom only carried out by primitive and godless tribes that inhabited the edges of the civilized world, i.e. the empire. It almost seemed as if the public did not regard the sailors as cannibals at all, as if such a thing was just an impossibility among an advanced and civilized people such as themselves.

All manner of other tales were exhumed by both sides in the debate. Perhaps the most famous example of seafaring cannibalism had been the case of a French frigate that went down en route to Senegal. The *Medusa* sank in 1816; 150 survivors clung to a makeshift raft that became a tiny floating hell. Vicious fights broke out over the few salvaged supplies and the weak and sick were killed and eaten. Only fifteen men survived the ordeal, which was immortalized in a vast painting by the French Romantic painter Géricault in 1819. Another, earlier, case was cited from a collection of medical curiosities compiled by the Dutch physician Nicolaas Tulp in 1641 (a man who was himself immortalized in Rembrandt's painting *Anatomy Lesson of Dr Nicolaas Tulp*). Tulp's tale was of seven English sailors adrift in the Caribbean. After seventeen days of drifting, one of them suggested drawing lots to decide who should be sacrificed for the others to live. It was agreed, and the man who had made the suggestion drew the short straw. He was systematically drained of blood and eaten. When the remaining six were finally washed ashore on the Dutch island of Saint Martin all charges against them were dropped on the grounds of unavoidable necessity.

The crew of the *Mignonette* were eventually found guilty of murder and sentenced to death, largely because the court had no choice but to act on the account that the men had freely given. The court also recommended that the sentence be commuted by the Crown, and this was duly done. Within a year of the wreck all three men were back in their homes having served just six months in prison. Captain Dudley later emigrated to Australia where he became one of the first victims of a plague outbreak in 1900.

It was in the same part of the world where Captain Dudley's diseased body was buried in a sulphur-filled coffin that another of the many faces of cannibalism came to light fifty years later. In 1950 Australian advisers in the remote eastern mountains of New Guinea came across a disease that was decimating the local people at an alarming rate. The people of the area, many of whom lived in a manner that had not altered since the Stone Age, called the disease "Kuru", which meant "the trembling". Its symptoms were well known and universally dreaded. First the victim started to lose coordination and found it increasingly difficult to walk. The hands and feet soon began to shake uncontrollably and eventually, after a period of up to six months, the victim would be unable to stand, speak or even swallow. Death usually came from starvation or pneumonia. D. C. Gajdusek, an American virus expert working in Australia, heard about the disease and decided to investigate. For years he studied the problem and collected data on every possible cause he could think of.

Gajdusek's first thought was that something must be attacking the brain and nervous system of the kuru victims – that much was clear from the progressive loss of motor control caused by the disease. Blood and tissue samples were collected and studied but revealed no known viruses. Gajdusek even took local soil samples to try and isolate any contaminants that may have been getting into the food chain – again with no result. Not only were attempts to isolate the cause of the disease a total failure, there was absolutely no success in finding a treatment. Antibiotics, vitamin supplements and mineral compounds all failed to produce any measurable effect on the progress of the disease. Eventually Gajdusek had to leave New Guinea, but he continued to worry at the problem. One day he read an article by a British scientist which pointed out the similarities between kuru and a disease of sheep known as scrapie. In both cases the victims suffer a progressive loss of motor control caused by degeneration of the brain. In scrapie the disease had been shown to be caused by a virus with an incubation period of several years.

Gajdusek returned to New Guinea, examined tissue samples from the brains of kuru victims and isolated the virus – work that won him the 1976 Nobel Prize for medicine. Although it was now known what caused kuru it still wasn't clear how the virus got from one victim to another. A short time later a husband and wife team of anthropologists named Glass came up with the answer. They discovered that kuru had long been present among the peoples of the area, but had always been restricted to a few cases in a generation. Gajdusek himself had noted that the local people spoke of a previous epidemic forty years before the one he was investigating. The Glasses discovered that in about 1915 the Fore tribe, the largest in the area, had taken up a form of ritual cannibalism. The muscles and major organs of the dead were roasted and eaten by surviving members of the family – one of the most important organs being the brain. Kuru was passed from brain to brain in the most direct way possible; by one person eating the dead brain of another. As in most cases of ritual cannibalism, the purpose of this grisly meal was to take in the wisdom and strength of an ancestor. The epidemic forty years earlier had died down because the Fores' cannibal practices had been stamped out by Christian missionaries and governors who were determined to civilize the so-called "barbarians" they found themselves among.

The medical insights gained from the study of kuru were later to prove valuable during the "Mad Cow" phenomenon of the early 1990s. Scientists immediately noticed the similarities with scrapie and kuru and were quick to isolate a long-incubation, brain-attacking virus. It was spread by feeding cows the boiled-down remains of the brains and spinal tissues of other cows; a kind of enforced cannibalism inflicted on natural herbivores. It was the fact that a similar disease existed in humans that persuaded governments that it may not be a good idea to allow meat that could be infected with any kind of brain virus to be sold.

The Green Children

· ·

Orphans of another world?

Tales of fairies and fairy children are part of a long and rich tradition of rural folklore. Since the earliest times, communities all over Europe have recognized certain places as powerful in the magic of the little or uncanny folk. Often these sites can be identified as prehistoric burial grounds or sites of ancient pagan worship. Dim recollections of the strange and timeless ceremonies that must have taken place at these locations in the long millennia before recorded history were preserved as local myths and legends of a supernatural people who lived in the trees and rocks and especially beneath the earth. Many of these sites are associated with real or imagined underground chambers and passages that were believed to give access to the underworld of the fairy people. The magic of the fairy people was often quirky and mischievous, and their power to cause chaos, good fortune or death was carefully respected. A fascinating case from the twelfth century that is intimately tied up with these beliefs involves two very strange children found near the English village of Woolpit in Suffolk.

In 1200 a monk and scribe by the name of William of Newburgh was the first to record the story of the green children of Woolpit. His account is found in part of an historical chronicle he wrote about the reign of King Stephen, which lasted from 1135 to 1154. Apart from this one incredible tale, the chronicle is a paradigm of straightforward and fair historical reporting. William of Newburgh is regarded as a reliable historical source by modern scholars, which makes his incredible story all the more compelling.

Nor does it seem right to pass over an unheard-of prodigy, which, as is well known, took place in England during the reign of King Stephen. Though it is asserted by many, yet I have long been in doubt concerning the matter, and deemed it ridiculous to give credit to a circumstance supported on no rational foundation, or at least one of a very mysterious character; yet, at length I was so overwhelmed by the weight of so many and such competent witnesses, that I have been compelled to believe, and wonder over a matter, which I was unable to comprehend, or unravel, by any powers of intellect.

In East Anglia there is a village, distant, as it is said, four or five miles from the noble monastery of the blessed king and martyr, Edmund; near this place are seen some very ancient cavities, called "Wolfpittes", that is, in English, "Pits for wolves", and which give their name to the adjacent village [Wulpet]. During harvest, while the reapers were employed in gathering in the produce of the fields, two children, a boy and a girl, completely green in their persons, and clad in garments of a strange colour, and unknown materials, emerged from these excavations.

The account goes on to describe how villagers discovered the children weeping among the long grass and managed to capture them although they seemed terrified and tried to run away. Dumbfounded by the children's extraordinary appearance, the villagers took them to the house of the local feudal lord, Sir Richard de Calne. Once there it was observed that it wasn't just the children's appearance that was inexplicable, they also behaved rather oddly. Another monastic chronicler, Abbot Ralph of Coggeshall, continues the story.

> *No one could understand their speech. When they were brought as curiosities to the house of a certain knight, Sir Richard de Calne, at Wikes, they wept bitterly. Bread and other victuals were set before them, but they would touch none of them, though they were tormented by great hunger, as the girl afterwards acknowledged. At length, when some beans just cut, with their stalks, were brought into the house, they made signs, with great avidity, that they should be given to them. When they were brought, they opened the stalks instead of the pods, thinking the beans were in the hollow of them; but not finding them there, they began to weep anew. When those who were present saw this, they opened the pods, and showed them the naked beans. They fed on these with delight, and for a long time tasted no other food.*

The green children of Woolpit continued to live in the house of Sir Richard. Abbot Ralph's account says that the boy soon sickened and died but that the girl grew strong and healthy and eventually lost her green hue after becoming accustomed to a more normal diet. He also records that the girl soon learned to speak English, was baptized and worked as a servant in her benefactor's house for many years until she married a man from King's Lynn in Norfolk. Once she had mastered the language the green girl, who seems to have never been given a name, was able to answer at least some of the questions that burned on everybody's tongue. Where did you come from, why did you come, how did you get here?

There are several versions of the green girl's explanation of her origins. No doubt she told the story a thousand times to a thousand different people and added or left out details as she remembered or forgot them. The essence of her story was that she and her brother had come from an entirely green world inhabited by green-skinned people and lit by a dim, watery green sun. She claimed that this world was far away, although she could not say where, and that the world she now inhabited was visible from there as a land of brilliant illumination on the other side of an uncrossable shining river or sea. One day she and her brother entered a cave they had not seen before. In some accounts she claimed they went into the cavern because they were chasing an animal and in others because they could hear the sound of bells ringing deep underground. Abbot Ralph ascribes their journey from one world to the next to the lure of the bells.

Being asked how she came into this country with the aforesaid boy, she replied that, as they were following their flocks, they came to a certain cavern, on entering which they heard a delightful sound of bells; ravished by whose sweetness, they went for a long time wandering on through the cavern, until they came to its mouth. When they came out of it, they were struck senseless by the excessive light of the sun, and the unusual temperature of the air; and they thus lay for a long time. Being terrified by the noise of those who came on them, they wished to fly, but they could not find the entrance of the cavern before they were caught.

William of Newburgh's explanation is similar, except that he adds that the land the children came from was called St Martin's land and that the people there were all Christian and built many churches.

Such an ancient and well-documented tale has attracted innumerable theories and interpretations over the years. It is clear that people at the time regarded the Woolpit children as denizens of the fairy realm who had somehow got lost and wandered into the world of mortals. The bizarre greenness of their skin, the unfamiliar material and cut of their clothes and the fact that they spoke a strange language all suggested to the superstitious medieval peasant an obvious connection with the underworld of the fairies. Modern commentators have attempted to explain the green children without resorting to the supernatural. Certain medical conditions related to jaundice and dietary deficiencies are known to produce a greenish hue to the skin that, once corrected, can disappear quickly. The fact that the boy died soon after he was discovered also suggests that their colour could have been due to an illness. The strange language spoken by the children could just have been a local dialect. In the twelfth century the

English language was nowhere near as uniform as it is today. Few people travelled and there was no national media – villages only a few miles apart could speak dialects so different that it would be hard to recognize them as based on the same language. The fact that the surviving girl picked up the new language so quickly might suggest that it wasn't actually all that different from her own. To the modern rationalist, then, the children were just lost, perhaps only a few miles from home and possibly suffering from a dietary deficiency. As reassuring as this theory is, it doesn't account for the green girl's own description of how she came to be in Woolpit.

A more revealing reading of the Woolpit legend emerges if you take into account some common beliefs of the time. Although England was officially a Christian kingdom by the time of King Stephen, Christianity had only been established for a few hundred years. A very small proportion of the population lived in cities at this time, most were still tied to the land as the virtual slaves of feudal landlords like Richard de Calne. This rural population lived in conditions that had changed very little since Celtic times a thousand years before. Their beliefs, although overlaid by Christian festivals and barely understood Christian theology, were essentially the same beliefs as their pagan ancestors had held. As we have already seen, a belief in the underworld was prominent among them.

The underworld was the place of the dead – it was later adopted by Christianity as hell. Tales of heroes descending into the underworld to rescue wives or friends are commonplace throughout European folklore – the tale of Eurydice is a classic example from

Greek myth. It was also the place where souls waited to be born into the world. With this in mind, the green girl's description of her journey takes on a whole new meaning. The land of dim twilight on the other side of the caverns she emerged from can be seen as the underworld of the dead or the yet to be born. The bright, illuminated land on the other side of the brilliant river can be seen as the land of the living that souls in the underworld long to reach. The whole narrative of passing through a tunnel from a dark, twilight world to a world of startling brilliance and sunshine can be read as a description of birth.

So, is the Woolpit children story no more than a medieval pagan allegory for birth and death? Perhaps, although it seems odd that a Christian monk would include it in an historical chronicle unless he regarded it as a real event. Perhaps William and Ralph had heard the story and simply not understood its symbolic meaning. There is another intriguing possibility; the discovery of the Woolpit children could easily have been a real event – orphans, strays and runaways were common in those dangerous and brutal times. Their green colour could be explained by a medical condition or perhaps they were just covered in green lichen and moss that had rubbed off the walls of the caverns as they hid there. Their craving for a particular food, in this case beans, is a common reaction among people suffering from dietary deficiencies. If the green girl really existed, her early experiences must have had a profound effect on her. Whatever traumatic event led to her becoming lost or abandoned in the first place, followed by the death of her brother, must have acted powerfully on her mind. Perhaps as she grew up she came to believe that she really was from St Martin's land and began to embroider the story as she told it over and over. Perhaps she was well aware of the symbolic significance of what she was saying, and used it to create an aura of mystery around herself that would ensure she was never ignored or abandoned again.

The Stone Age Astronomers

••••••••••••••••••••••••••••••••••••

Who told the Dogon about Sirius?

In 1951 two French anthropologists, Marcel Griaule and Germaine Dieterlen, published an article in an obscure scientific journal called *Journal de la Société d'Africainistes*. The paper was entitled "A Sudanese Sirius System" and attracted almost no attention, even among anthropology specialists. In the years since its publication, however, a number of writers and researchers have come across the paper and declared it to contain information that could revolutionize the way we think about the early history of human civilization. Among these writers is the Swiss author Erich von Dänikan, who has astonished the world with his claims that the Earth has played host to a series of visits by advanced extraterrestrial civilizations and that ancient cultures have recorded these visits.

The subject of Griaule and Dieterlen's paper was the mythology of an African people known as the Dogon. There are about a quarter of a million Dogon scattered in and around the Hombori Mountains of the west African nation of Mali. Marcel Griaule first visited these extraordinary people in 1931 while on a scientific expedition in what was then the French colony of Sudan. Over the next few years he became fascinated by their complex and strange mythology which was quite unlike anything else he had come across in Africa. Griaule lived among the Dogon and recorded their myths, many of which seemed to be bound up with a deep understanding of astronomy. In 1946 he visited the Dogon again, this time in the company of Germaine Dieterlen. Now fully accepted, Griaule was finally initiated into the secret rites of the tribe and gained access to their inexplicable knowledge.

If you look into the eastern sky on a clear night in August you will see a star that outshines all the others. This is Sirius, also known as the "Dog star". Sirius is the brightest star visible from the southern hemisphere and Griaule was not overly surprised to find that it was the centre of Dogon mythology. What astonished him was the detailed knowledge the Dogon possessed about an object that is almost nine light years away (82.5 billion kilometres). To the naked eye, Sirius looks like any other star, although a little brighter. In fact, like many of the stars visible from Earth, Sirius is a binary system – it consists of two stars orbiting one another very closely. Because of the great distances involved, binary stars look like a single point of light unless examined with a very powerful telescope. What grabbed Griaule's attention was the fact that the Dogon knew that Sirius had a companion star – knowledge that western scientists had only learned in 1862. Not only that, but the Dogon told Griaule that they knew this because people from Sirius had visited their forefathers many thousands of years ago.

Sirius is classed as a first-magnitude star (the brightest class). It is situated in the constellation of Canis Major and has long been an object of interest to astronomers. In the 1830s the astronomer Friedrich

Bessel noticed that the movement of Sirius across the sky was irregular, and proposed that the gravitational pull of another massive body close to it must be the cause of these fluctuations. After twelve years of study Bessel had enough data to prove that something was indeed affecting the motion of Sirius. Although this second object could not be seen with even the most powerful telescopes of the day, Bessel was convinced it was there and named it Sirius B. In 1862 an American, Alvan Clarke, finally confirmed the existence of Sirius B using his own forty-seven-centimetre telescope. Sirius B is a white dwarf – a small but incredibly dense star that gives off very little light. So, while Sirius is one of the brightest objects in the sky – it's thirty-five times bigger and brighter than our own sun and relatively close in astronomical terms – Sirius B is one of the dimmest and it's only about twice as big as the Earth. The discovery of Sirius B is often cited as a classic example of the power of modern science, and yet it appears that the Dogon knew all about it while Europeans were still living in caves.

According to Dogon mythology a people called the Nommo came to Earth from Sirius aeons ago and were worshipped by the Dogon as gods. The Nommo landed in a massive spinning craft that descended on a pillar of flame and kicked up a huge dust storm as it came down at a location to the north of where the Dogon now live. The Nommo were like fish and lived in water on their home world – a planet that orbits Sirius in the same direction as Sirius B. It's worth bearing in mind that Griaule heard this description of a remarkably modern-sounding alien encounter in 1946 – long before today's familiar images of UFOs. The Dogon claim that there are four bodies in orbit around Sirius;

Sirius B (which they name Digitaria), a large, light-weight planet known as Emme Ya, a moon of Emme Ya (called the "star of women"), and a planet named Shoemaker that orbits in the opposite direction to all the other companions of Sirius. The very fact that the Dogon speak of bodies spinning and orbiting in space would be incredible on its own were it not for their even more precise knowledge of these bodies.

Knowledge of the Sirius star system eight and a half light years away is not the only startling aspect of Dogon lore. Their legends say that the Moon is "dry and dead", that Saturn has a ring around it (this is only visible with a powerful telescope) and that Jupiter has four major moons. In Dogon temples the orbit of Venus is recorded with remarkable accuracy and they say that the stars are infinite in number. All of this knowledge they attribute to the Nommo. The one aspect of the Dogon's story that does not ring true is their description of the Nommo landing site. The area in which the Dogon lives in tremendously arid and rocky – why would an amphibious people like the Nommo choose a semi-desert region as a landing place? The writer Robert Temple has suggested that the Dogon's knowledge may in fact have come from the ancient Egyptian civilization – Egypt is a short distance north-west of Mali.

Temple claims that the Egyptians also possessed this information but that it perished with their civilization. Sirius was certainly worshipped by the Egyptians, its first appearance in the sky heralded the life-giving flood waters of the Nile. The star was represented by Sothis, god of the rising waters, and associated with the powerful goddess Isis. Temple points out that Isis is often shown in a boat with two other goddesses,

Summary of Dogon traditions about Sirius compared with modern astronomical knowledge

Sirius has a companion star named Digitaria.

Sirius is orbited by a companion star named Sirius B.

Digitaria is small but massively heavy and determines the position of Sirius.

Sirius B is a massively dense white dwarf that significantly alters the motion of Sirius.

Digitaria orbits Sirius once every fifty years.

Sirius B orbits Sirius every 50.04 years.

Digitaria is invisible.

Sirius B is a ninth magnitude star only visible through a powerful telescope.

Digitaria revolves around itself in less than a year.

Rotational speed of Sirius B is unknown to science.

There are two planets and at least one moon orbiting Sirius.

The existence of thirty-one planets outside the solar system have been confirmed, none have yet been detected in the Sirius system. Until twenty years ago many scientists doubted the existence of planets around stars other than our sun.

Anukis and Satis, and takes this to show that the Egyptians knew Sirius to be a three-star system. Other mythologies also make reference to powerful, amphibious gods. Babylonian myth claims an amphibian ruler named Oannes as the founder of their civilization.

Whether the source of the Dogons' knowledge was extraterrestrial or whether they obtained it second hand from a more powerful civilization, the fact that they clearly possessed knowledge of things that they could not possibly have seen for themselves is one of the world's most compelling mysteries. As our knowledge of the universe slowly expands we will one day be able to say for sure if the, as yet, unproven aspects of Dogon knowledge are also true. If they are, the mystery can only deepen.

Trepanation Trepidation

* *

You need it like a hole in the head

The International Trepanation Advocacy Group (ITAG) is a well-organized and professional association based in Sweden. They have an informative and well-designed website, regular periodicals and a dedicated staff. Listed on the itinerary of a medical conference or meeting of international charities they would probably go unnoticed by most people – unless they happened to know the meaning of "trepanation". This rather dull-sounding organization is dedicated to promoting the practice of drilling holes in the skulls of healthy, sane adults all over the world. It should quickly be added that the owners of these skulls are to be wholly in agreement with the procedure and first brought to an understanding of the considerable health benefits it can bring. In an age of healing crystals, aromatherapy kits on the high street and bizarre fad diets, the ITAG may sound like just another group of, particularly extreme, New Age health freaks, but their views are based on a well-documented medical practice that has been carried out all over the world for thousands of years.

The word "trepanation", comes from the Greek *trypanon*, meaning "a borer", and dates from classical times. The bone drill used in modern brain surgery of the more orthodox kind is known as a trepan. It is used to give surgeons access to the brain and to relieve pressure inside the skull caused by internal bleeding or infection. Evidence that people were carrying out similar operations in the Stone Age has been turning up since the earliest days of archaeological research. Skulls found all across Europe, and particularly in the Danube basin, were found to have regular holes bored into them by some kind of man-made tool. At first it was thought that these holes must have been the result of wounds received in battle, or even during primitive executions in which the victim was gruesomely killed by having a gaping hole bored through his head and into his brain. Closer study revealed that in many examples this could not have been the case. The holes were too smooth and regular to have been caused by any known weapon and in some skulls there were more than one. Medical experts who examined the strange wounds pointed out that a lot of them showed signs of having healed after the hole had been made – the edges of the orifices were fused in a way character-istic of healing bone. This clearly showed that the holes had been made while the person was alive, and that they had survived for several years after the operation had been carried out. Archaeologists began to realize that they were dealing with evidence of a deliberate and careful medical procedure rather than a brutal wounding.

An early example of this process of scientific deduction can be traced to a skull found at a Stone Age burial site in southern France. The archaeologist who found the skull surmised that a large piece had been sawn off the cranium in order to turn the skull into a drinking vessel. He also noted that the edge of the cut had been polished and "expressly made for the application of the lips". This theory was totally in keeping with scientific opinion of the time which held that our cave-dwelling ancestors had been nothing but blood-thirsty savages. Some time later the skull came into the hands of Professor Paul Broca in Paris. Broca was an expert in cranial anatomy and noticed that the so called "polished edges" had actually been smoothed by the process of bone healing. In Broca's time medical experiments in which the skulls' of patients were perforated to gain access to the brain almost always resulted in the death of the patient, yet he had evidence that "primitive" doctors had been performing the same operation with complete success thousands of years before.

Evidence began to accumulate from all around the world. Skulls from peoples who had lived in South America long before the time of Columbus showed exactly the same features. The skull of an Inca from Cuzco had no less than seven bore holes, at least some of which were made on different occasions. A particu-larly fascinating and initially puzzling find was made in Dorset, England. A 4000-year-old skull with a circular section about eight centimetres in diameter cut out of it was unearthed from Crichel Down. Oddly, the removed section was found with the skull, although bone healing showed that the owner of the skull had survived the operation by several years. The implica-tion is that the patient had kept the section that had been removed from his head and had it buried with him when he died – perhaps an indication of an early belief in reincarnation which required that the body be whole in the grave.

Quite apart from these archaeological finds, anthro-pologists working in remote regions of the world found many peoples who were still practising trepanation well into the twentieth century. In 1829 William Ellis, a missionary to the northenmost of the southern Pacific islands, reported that trepanation was carried out by the local people. The procedure involved scraping into the skull of an injured or sick person until the brain was exposed and then sealing the hole with a piece of coconut shell. Ellis also stated that victims of skull fractures were treated in the same way and that sometimes parts of the brain were removed and replaced with pig's brain!

In a paper punchily entitled "Trepanation of the Skull by the Medicine-men of Primitive Cultures, with Particular Reference to Present-day Native East African Practice", Dr Edward Margetts documented examples of peoples known to have been practising trepanation right up until the first half of the twentieth century. He listed groups from North and South America, the Pacific Islands, central Asia and Africa. Margetts was particularly interested in the Kisii and Tende peoples of east Africa where trepanation was a widely accepted treatment for everything from persistent headaches to skull fracture. One man's experience of the procedure forms the most interesting section of Margetts's paper.

The man, who was about fifty years old in 1958, was known as "Hat On, Hat Off" . He habitually wore a battered old brown hat and, as long as he kept his hat on, looked perfectly normal. When the hat came off, however, the effect was breathtaking, so much of his skull had been removed that it looked like the top quarter of his head was missing. Hat On, Hat Off, or Hat On as he was known to his friends, had been a policeman in 1945 when he had cracked his head on a door frame and developed persistent headaches. The tribal doctor recommended trepanation and over the next seven years Hat On had between five and thirty operations – he found it hard to remember – that left him with about ninety square centimetres of skull missing. He never complained of headaches again. The man who operated on Hat On had been carrying out trepanations for over fifty years and had learned the craft from his father before him. His main tool was a curved and wickedly sharp knife that he used to scrape through the bone. Other doctors in the area used saws and drills which he disapproved of and said would never catch on.

Archaeologists and anthropologists have now identified four main methods of trepanation. Celtic and Norse surgeons from around 300 AD had fine metal knives and scrapers not dissimilar to the ones used in east Africa. It was probably from these people that the Romans learned the technique. In south and north America, where metal work was practically unknown before Columbus, surgeons used implements of obsidian – a hard, black volcanic rock that splits with a razor's edge. Similar tools made of flint or mussel shells were probably used by prehistoric Europeans. The ancient Greeks and Arabs used a very fine drill to make a ring of holes that were then joined together with a saw to create a removable bone section. In some parts of the world the operation appears to have been carried out rather more directly with a sharp chisel and heavy mallet.

In the case of Hat On, trepanation was a cure for headaches. In most cases in ancient times it was probably carried out as a treatment for head wounds received in battle. It has been pointed out that most

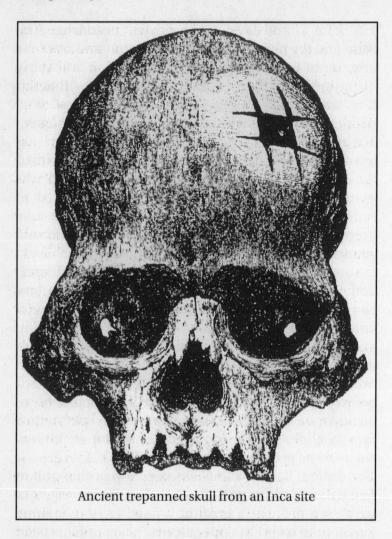

Ancient trepanned skull from an Inca site

trepanned skulls have a section removed from the left side, the most likely site of a head injury inflicted by a right-handed opponent, and belong to males. In China and India there is a long tradition of boring into the skull to remove "worms" or "beetles" from the brain.

Medieval Chinese texts mention Ta-Chhin from Syria who had the skill of removing dangerous worms from the brain. Indian texts record the exploits of Atreya "King of Physicians" who taught the art of curing blindness by opening the skull and extracting worms. Modern doctors have speculated that these "worms" may have been parasitic tapeworm larvae which are known to lodge in the brain and grow until they cause pressure that can lead to headaches, blindness and eventual death.

There are other, less scientific, explanations for trepanation however. It is not difficult to imagine our pagan ancestors attributing headaches, nosebleeds, fits or persistent unconsciousness to a bad spirit trapped in the skull. The obvious way to let the spirit out would be to drill a hole in the head. People capable of carrying out this operation, and thereby saving the patient's life as well as his sanity, must have been held in very high regard. Probably they were the shamans or witch doctors who looked after their people's spiritual as well as physical well-being. Some advocates of trepanation today believe that having a hole in your cranium is actually beneficial to general mental and physical health. They point out that the skulls of infants are soft and able to flex with the heartbeat and accommodate brain development. Within a few months, however, the skull becomes rigid, creating a fixed cranial environment that severely limits mental development. The idea of the third eye, taken from Asian philosophy, is often brought up. The third eye is an energy point in the middle of the forehead used as a focus of concentration in meditation and said to be the channel through which psychic energies can flow. This point has become a favourite drill-site for modern day trepanners.

All members of the International Trepanation Advocacy Group proudly boast that they have been trepanned. Because very few surgeons will carry out the procedure without a very good medical reason, most have to resort to self-trepanation, often with home power tools. The ITAG states very strongly that it does not advocate self-trepanation and urges those interested in the procedure to think carefully and seek expert medical advice. They even provide a sample agreement absolving a doctor of responsibility in case anybody decides to pursue the idea further.

The Ancient Map Makers

●●●●●●●●●●●●●●●●●●●●●●●●●●●●●●●●●●

A lost maritime civilization

One dull afternoon in 1956 a cartographer named Walters was leafing through a set of dusty old maps at the US Navy Hydrographic Office when he came across something rather extraordinary. Among the tattered old parchments was a map that had been given to the office by a Turkish naval officer. It was dated 919 by the Muslim calendar, about 1513 according to Western reckoning. At 450 years old it was certainly a rare document but by no means the oldest map in existence. What was so extraordinary, however, was its remarkable accuracy. It showed the north coast of Africa and the entire coast of South America in great detail. A quick check also revealed that it showed the coastline of these continents at precisely the correct longitude and latitude. Considering the date, this was unbelievable.

The American continent had been known about for less than twenty years in 1513 and other maps of the period are glaringly inaccurate, even about the geography of Europe let alone the largely unexplored New World – one of the most accurate land maps of the period shows Spain joined to Italy! These were remarkable enough findings but there were still more stunning revelations. The map clearly showed a land mass to the south that looked a lot like Antarctica – a

continent that was not supposed to have been discovered until 1818. It also showed a ridge running north
to south through the mid-Atlantic. Walters and any
other modern cartographer would have known that
such a ridge does indeed exist – it's a major volcanic
feature a mile beneath the waves on the sea bed! How
could an early sixteenth-century map maker have
known so much about the world's geography at a time
when it was only tentatively being explored, and how
could he have known about features on the ocean
floor that were not discovered until 400 years later?

The map that Walters had been studying is known as
the Piri Re'is map. It was made by a Turkish pirate who
had been executed in 1554. Despite his occupation Piri
Re'is had held high office in the Ottoman Empire and
was known to historians as a governor of Egypt.
Documents have survived in which Re'is describes
making the map by copying parts of twenty other maps
that were themselves copies of maps from the Library
of Alexandria. This legendary institution had been
founded by Alexander the Great to house all the
knowledge of the world. It was destroyed by fire in
640 AD along with most of the knowledge of the ancient
world. Many historians and scholars would gladly give
a limb to learn just one of the secrets that the great
Library of Alexandria held, and now here was a map
compiled from ancient documents held in that very
library. In fact, there was another copy of the Piri Re'is
map in the US Library of Congress where it had been
since it was "discovered" in a museum in Istanbul.
Until Walters came along though nobody had paid it
much attention or noticed its significance.

Walters showed his map to Allington Mallery, a
retired captain and expert on antique sea charts, who

agreed to look it over. After careful and sceptical study Mallery made another startling discovery. He confirmed that the southern land mass was indeed Antarctica and, what is more, that it showed the coastline of the continent that lies beneath the mile-thick ice sheets that cover the area today. Mallery only knew this because of pioneering work carried out by a scientific expedition in 1949. Using sonar, the joint Swedish, British and Norwegian team had managed to map the actual coast of Queen Maud Land far beneath the ice. Mallery noted that the expedition's findings and the Antarctic coastline indicated on the Piri Re'is map were apparently identical. How could an ancient map maker have known the coastline of a continent that modern science had only been able to map in the mid-twentieth century?

According to our very incomplete understanding of global climate, the Earth goes through cycles of cooling and warming at intervals of a few thousand years. During warm periods, a large proportion of the ice at the poles melts, probably leaving much of Antarctica exposed. During cold periods, the ice sheets advance, covering huge areas of ocean in the south and much of Europe, North America and Northern Asia in the north. Even today scientists are not sure if the Earth is heading into a cold period or emerging from one, but they do agree that the most recent time that Antarctica could have been ice free is at least 6000 years ago. If the Piri Re'is map shows an accurate representation of the Antarctic coast beneath the ice then there are two equally startling conclusions. Either map makers at the time of Alexander the Great possessed a technology for seeing through ice, like sonar, or the map makers of the time were themselves copying even more ancient maps – maps made when the poles were ice free, at least 6000 years ago.

In the early 1960s Walters and Mallery's research came into the hands of the writer Charles Hapgood who, in 1966, published a book entitled *Maps of the Ancient Sea Kings* which took the Piri Re'is map as a starting point and added a wealth of further investigations. Hapgood gained access to a large number of ancient maps held at the Library of Congress and came across some more startling finds. He found a number of maps used by seafarers during the Middle Ages that had been largely ignored by historians. Many of them had features similar to the Piri Re'is map – they showed land masses that should not have been known about at the times the maps were made and they did this with incredible accuracy. How could medieval seaman have created such accurate maps when we know they did not even have the instruments to measure longitude and latitude properly? Hapgood was convinced that these maps were based on ancient Greek examples and he found some compelling evidence.

In the year 240 BC the Greek scientist Eratosthanes knew that the Earth was a sphere and set out to find its circumference. He based his calculation on observations he made in Egypt. At Syrene he noticed that the sun was directly overhead at midday on 21 June and cast no shadows. However, at Alexandria on the same date at midday the sun cast shadows at 7.5 degrees. Eratosthanes knew the distance from Alexandria to Syrene and from this was able to calculate the amount of curvature of the Earth's surface between these two points, by extrapolating the result he came up with a figure for the entire circumference of the planet. Due to a small error in the measured distance between

Syrene and Alexandria, Eratosthanes overestimated the Earth's circumference by about 4.5 per cent – nevertheless this was a remarkable achievement when you consider that 1700 years later most Europeans believed the world was flat. Hapgood noticed that if he subtracted Eratosthanes's 4.5 per cent error from the Piri Re'is map it became even more accurate.

Hapgood argued that the Alexandrian map makers copied older maps on to a sphere that was 4.5 per cent too large, resulting in the small errors that showed up in Re'is's copy centuries later. These ancient Greek scholars were simply using the most up-to-date model of the world – Eratosthanes's calculation – to correct what they assumed to be errors in the even more ancient maps they were copying. In fact, the maps they were copying were based on a model of the world that was more accurate than their own. Where did these maps come from and who could have made them?

Hapgood found another clue among the labyrinth of mystery that is ancient Egyptian history. According to tradition, the base of the Great Pyramid is supposed to be exactly one eighth of a minute of a degree of the Earth's circumference. Hapgood checked the figures and found the result to be significantly more accurate than the figure produced by Eratosthanes in 240 BC. The Great Pyramid was built in about 2500 BC. If it isn't just a coincidence that its base is almost exactly one eighth of a degree of a minute of arc – and given that ancient Egyptians had an obsession with sacred geometry this seems unlikely – then somebody had a way of measuring the Earth's circumference at least 2200 years before Eratosthanes was born. Presumably these were the same people who made the maps that have been copied down the centuries. We know that the Egyptians were not great mariners or explorers, their civilization was insular and obsessed with a rigid religious hierarchy that placed far more importance on the next world than in the present. It seems highly unlikely that they were the great explorers who had made these maps, probably this was knowledge they had inherited from another, older civilization. Another point that argues against the Egyptians as the ancient map makers is Mallery's observation that the Piri Re'is map shows Antarctica free of ice. The year 2500 BC is just not early enough for such conditions to have existed. The original must have been made at least 1500 years before the Great Pyramid was built.

Among the other documents studied by Hapgood was another Turkish map made in 1550. Not only does it show the world with incredible accuracy, it appears to have been based on an original made at a time when Asia and North America were still connected by a land bridge. Modern geologists estimate that the last time these conditions existed was about 12,000 years ago. The Siberia-Alaska land bridge existed because sea levels were much lower in the remote past. This was one of the Earth's cold periods when much of the world's water was frozen at the poles. Other maps found by Hapgood seem to show northern Europe covered by ice sheets, again indicating that they were made during the last ice age 12,000 years ago. Could people have been sailing the oceans with sophisticated navigation equipment that long ago? Perhaps Hapgood's most thought-provoking discovery was a Chinese map from the twelfth century AD. He was astonished to discover that it had the same 4.5 per cent error that he had found in European and Middle

Eastern maps. Hapgood was now looking at the possibility of an ancient seafaring race with worldwide influence.

It's a remarkable and little realized fact that we know almost nothing about the long history of humanity. For hundreds of thousands of years people just like us have lived on Earth. Our detailed knowledge of what our ancestors did and said extends back about 2000 years. Beyond that there are patches of good knowledge that quickly peter out into millennia upon millennia of pure guesswork. There is no reason to believe that our ancient ancestors were any less capable or daring than we are – the instinct to build and explore are clearly innate in us. In recent years, for example, archaeologists have confirmed the ancient legend that Vikings visited North America centuries before Columbus. Anthropologists also believe that a people of the south seas made incredible voyages that enabled them to colonize islands from Polynesia to New Zealand, and perhaps even South America. Who can say what else was achieved in those aeons of unrecorded history?

Hapgood was content to conclude that a seafaring race, with substantial ocean-going vessels and a highly accurate method of navigation, was exploring the globe at a time when conventional wisdom says people never sailed more than a few miles from the coast. Others have taken Hapgood's findings to prove everything from the existence of the legendary Atlantian civilization to the arrival of extraterrestrial visitors to Earth. Some believe that the presence of Antarctica on these ancient maps indicates that this was the home of the ancient map makers and is itself the lost continent of Atlantis. Until science comes up with a far more effective way of looking through the polar ice, or the ice itself disappears, we cannot carry out an archaeological survey of that vast continent – few archaeologists today believe there is a reason to. Others have claimed that the lack of archaeological evidence for the ancient map makers proves that the information for the maps must have come from an advanced extraterrestial race that visited the Earth and gave the results of their orbital surveys to the primitive inhabitants.

Since the original maps are lost, along with the ancient copies that Piri Re'is and others saw in the Library of Alexandria, we will never know for certain who created them or when. Whatever the answers to these question might have proved to be, it cannot be doubted that these obscure documents show that people in the distant past knew far more about the world than we give them credit for. Considering that our own civilization has had a true picture of the world for less than 500 years, perhaps this modern prejudice is understandable. For us the voyages of discovery made in the sixteenth and seventeenth centuries are still a source of pride, they are part of the folklore of the triumph of the sciences that we rely on so heavily today. But is it really so impossible that in all those aeons of lost, unrecorded time other people have not done what we have done, and perhaps unimaginably more?

The Bog Killers

Ancient rituals of death

Life on the cold, boggy, northern plains of Europe was not easy 2000 years ago. In areas that now lie within some of the world's safest and wealthiest countries, from Germany and Denmark to Great Britain and Ireland, wild hardy peoples struggled to survive in a bitter and unforgiving landscape. This was the millennium that saw the transition from the Bronze Age to the Iron Age in northern Europe, about 500 BC to 500 AD.

The peoples of this area were regarded with fear and loathing by the comfortable denizens of the Roman Empire that then dominated southern Europe – and not without good reason. These widely dispersed but numerous tribes represented a constant threat to the security of the empire's northern borders. More than once failed crops and harsh winters had driven hordes of these wild men bent on plunder into the very heart of the empire's rich farmlands. The great Roman historian Tacitus wrote about the peoples of this area in his book *Germania*. His descriptions of dark and terrifying fertility rituals involving human sacrifice have become so deeply embedded in the popular imagination down the ages that they were dismissed by scholars as horror stories without any basis in fact. That is until gruesome evidence that they were a reality began to turn up from beneath the earth.

For thousands of years the peoples of northern Europe have relied on peat as a cheap and widely available fuel source. Until well into the twentieth century peat was still used in remote rural communities and the practice of peat cutting was a part of everyday life. One chill and foggy April day in 1952 men from the Danish village of Grauballe were cutting the peat when one of them made a horrifying discovery. His spade wedged into a buried obstruction with a sickening crunch. Clearing away the thick, fibrous soil, he uncovered a human head and shoulders. The first thought of the peat cutters was murder. The body they had uncovered looked as if it had been dead only a matter of weeks – the skin was smooth and brown and its hair was short and reddish. Police and the local doctor, an amateur archaeologist, investigated. The body didn't match descriptions of any recent missing person and the doctor noticed that the peat above the body was undisturbed – it had not been buried recently.

Dr Peter Glob, an expert in prehistory at the University of Aarhus, was called in to examine the find. His initial conclusions were startling. Given the depth under the peat at which the body was found, it must have been there for about 2000 years – the length of time it would have taken for several metres of peat to form over it. Dr Glob was sure that this was the body of an Iron Age man – it was not the first he had seen. If he was correct, the cause of death would turn out to be less than pleasant. Back at the university a minute investigation of the corpse began. One of the first discoveries confirmed Dr Glob's suspicions. The throat had not just been cut, it had been viciously hacked and stabbed from ear to ear. An expression of excruciating agony and fear was preserved on the twisted features of the face. Further investigation revealed that the unfortunate man's skull had been smashed and both his legs broken. Had this been an isolated case, archaeologists would almost certainly have concluded that Grauballe man had been the victim of a vicious murder or battle, but it was not.

Two years before the gruesome find at Grauballe, a similar body had been uncovered by peat cutters at nearby Tollund Fen. Around the corpse's neck archaeologists found a plaited leather noose – damage to the vertebrae suggested that he had been killed by hanging. The body of a man dug out of the peat at Borre Fen in 1946 had also been hanged – this time with a twisted hemp rope. The bodies of two women were found in the same area. One had a smashed skull and a broken leg, the face of the other had been pulverized and she had been partly scalped. There had been a great deal of confusion about these bodies, with many people believing them to be recent murder victims because they were not decomposed. By 1956 and the discovery of Grauballe man, however, science had advanced significantly and archaeologists were able to prove that the bog bodies were ancient.

Several clues supported this conclusion. The remarkable state of preservation of the bodies is due to the nature of the peat they were buried in. In a bog there are very low levels of oxygen and very high levels of tannic acid. Under these conditions few of the microorganisms in the soil that break down organic matter can survive. The bodies were preserved as if they had been subjected to a leather tanning process – a fact evident from the tan-brown colour of the skin. These processes were a boon to the archaeologists. Radiocarbon dating of pieces of Grauballe man's liver and muscle tissue placed his death at 310 AD, plus or minus a century. Perfectly preserved pollen grains found in the same layer of peat as the body were from types of plants known to have thrived in the area before 400 BC. There could be no doubt that Grauballe man and the others had died at least 1500 years before they were discovered. But who were these unfortunate individuals and why did they meet with such gruesome deaths?

The bodies at Grauballe and Tollund were naked and no artefacts were found near them that might have given a clue to their identities (the Tollund body was wearing an unremarkable leather cap). Closer examination of the bodies provided a few clues. The hands were smooth and showed no sign of hard manual work – very unusual considering the society they had come from. By opening up the gut it was discovered that both men's last meal had been some form of vegetable gruel containing at least sixty types of plants and herbs. Preparation of such a meal must have been very complex and time-consuming and the large number of wild herbs suggests some kind of ritual or even magical concoction. In the case of the women's bodies there were some more concrete clues. These bodies had been partially covered by cloths and cut lengths of birch branches were found on or around them. One of the Borre Fen women was found with the bones of an infant and fragments of a clay pot. These differences suggested that the men and the women had been the victims of two different kinds of killing.

In his *Germania* Tacitus describes a chilling ritual carried out by the wild tribes beyond the empire's borders. For the people of these harsh regions spring was the most vital time of the year. The return of fertility

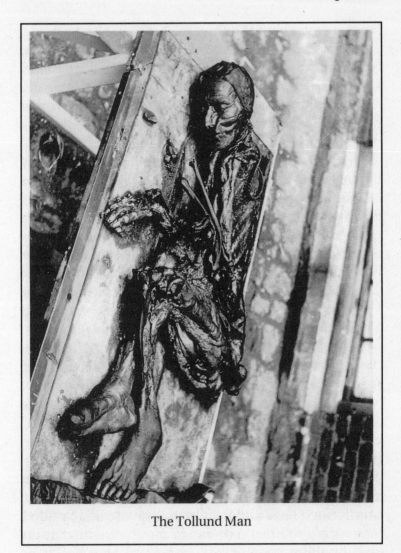

The Tollund Man

to the land after the extreme hardship of the winter months was the focus of their primitive religion. For these people only a goddess could be responsible for this annual miracle, and they named her Nerthus.

Tacitus describes a ritual associated with Nerthus:

> *They believe that she takes part in human affairs, riding on a chariot among her people. On an island in the sea stands a sacred grove in which there is a veiled chariot that no one but a high priest can touch. The priest senses the presence of the goddess among this grove and attends her as her chariot is drawn by sacred cows. There follow days of rejoicing and celebration in the places she visits and stays in. No one goes to war, no one takes up arms and every iron object is hidden away. Only then is there peace in the land, until the goddess grows tired of the company of men and is restored to her sacred grove by the priest. Then the chariot, the vestments and the goddess herself are cleansed in a sacred lake. This service is performed by slaves who are immediately afterwards drowned in the lake.*

Dr Glob and others have interpreted this ancient account to fit in with what was found in Denmark's bogs. He believes that these processions really took place and that their climax was the human sacrifice of a man who was chosen to be the husband of the goddess for the year, their mystical union ensuring the fertility of the land. Dr Glob speculated that the murdered men had been thrown into sacred lakes that later formed bogs and peat beds. The use of a braided rope recalls braided patterns found in ornamentation used by these peoples and associated with braids of corn or wheat that symbolized the goddess. The fact that the men had not worked for some time before their deaths suggests that they were either prisoners or perhaps willing volunteers who were treated like royalty in the months before the sacred sacrifice.

Perhaps their strange final meal contained herbal drugs that made them believe they were about to be united with Nerthus herself – ancient peoples are known to have used powerful mind-altering substances during religious ceremonies. On the Danish island of Zealand archaeologists have found four-wheeled wagons or chariots buried in the bogs. These chariots are delicately made and beautifully decorated, they also have a single "throne", perhaps to seat the goddess or her image. Dr Glob sees these as even more concrete evidence that the rituals Tacitus describes actually took place, and that the bodies in the bogs were their victims.

Further research has revealed the bodies found in the 1940s and 1950s were by no means the first to be dug out of the peat. For hundreds of years people have been coming across these strange, preserved bodies but it was not until the twentieth century that science began to take an interest. It's not hard to imagine the fear and horror these twisted corpses, stained the colour of the earth from which they emerged, must have aroused in the superstitious rural peoples of past centuries. Usually they were regarded as devils and burned. Sometimes they were recognized as men and women and given a Christian reburial. They were rarely studied and were only recorded, if at all, as objects of curiosity. Nevertheless, evidence has been gathered that at least 150 bodies have been given up by the peat bogs of northern Europe since the eighteenth century. Unfortunately, of those few that were reburied away from the preservative qualities of the bog, nothing remains to be studied.

But if the bog men were the husbands of the goddess, who were the women? Dr Glob suspects that their fate was less noble. Again it is Tacitus who describes how women condemned for unfaithfulness, and those guilty of cowardice or desertion or other "shameful" crimes, were pressed down into the bog under a wicker cage. The cut lengths of birch found in association with the women's bodies come chillingly to mind. Another female body found in Bred Fen in 1942 was bound hand and foot but otherwise uninjured. In the Eckernförde region peat cutters found the naked body of a fourteen-year-old girl. Her eyes had been blindfolded and a heavy rock used to drag her body down into the bog. Until recently it was a common belief in northern Europe that after a witch had been killed she must be fixed to the ground with a birch stake to stop her rising from the dead – perhaps a distant memory of the terrible punishments meted out by our Iron Age ancestors.

Recorded bog body finds

When   Where   Who   Details

1952
Grauballe, Denmark
Male
Complete naked body. Death by blows to the head and stab wounds to the throat.

1952
Windeby Bog, Germany
Female
Complete naked body. Hand, feet and eyes bound. Large rock used to sink body into the bog. Head shaved on left side. Long rods found on body.

1952
Windeby Bog, Germany
Male
Complete naked body. Death by choking with a hazel rod. Body pinned down with forked branches.

1950
Tollund Fen, Denmark
Male
Complete naked body. Death by hanging – braided leather rope in place around neck. Found wearing a leather cap and belt.

1948
Osterby, Germany
Male
Severed head wrapped in deerskin cape. Hair tied in Swabian knot described by Roman writers.

1948
Borre Fen, Denmark
Female
Complete naked body. Death by severe blows to the face. Found with a belted skirt.

1947
Borre Fen, Denmark
Female
Complete naked body. Death by severe blows to the skull. Found with a shawl and blanket and bronze and amber ornaments around the neck. Bones of an infant found nearby. Short sticks lay on the body.

1946
Borre Fen, Denmark
Male

Complete naked body. Death by hanging – hemp rope in place around neck. Found with two rolls of sheepskin and a cut birch branch.

1942
Bred Fen, Denmark
Female
Complete naked body. Death by drowning – body uninjured but tied hand and foot and wrapped in a cloth. Found wearing a woollen bonnet with her hair elaborately coiled about her head.

1942
Sígard Fen, Denmark
Male
Complete naked body. Cause of death unknown. Found wrapped in three leather capes and lying on a bed of bog-cotton – a plant associated with rebirth.

1879
Huldre Bog, Denmark
Female
Complete clothed body. Cause of death unknown. Found wearing check shirt. Willow stake lay on her breast.

1790
Bunsok, Germany
Male
Complete naked body. Found completely caged by willow sticks.

1773
South-west Denmark
Male
Complete naked body. Death by throat slashing. Hands tied behind back and short sticks placed on the body.

The Adam and Eve Generation

....

It had to start somewhere

Mankind has always been defenceless in the face of the more violent phenomena of nature. Even today we can do next to nothing to defend ourselves from the tremendous destructive power of tornadoes, volcanoes, earthquakes or tidal waves. It is by no means unusual to hear about the deaths of tens of thousands of people in an earthquake, or a flood that leaves millions homeless and destitute. The human race has lived with these disasters since its very beginnings and some of them, hidden in the depths of prehistory, must have been more terrible than anything we can imagine. Perhaps a few have been so terrible that they came close to wiping out the human race, and perhaps the memory of these appalling catastrophes have been passed down to us in myth and legend.

> *And God said unto Noah, The end of all flesh is come before me; for the earth is filled with violence through them; and, behold, I will destroy them with the earth . . . And the LORD said unto Noah, Come thou and all thy house into the ark; for thee have I seen righteous before me in this generation . . . And*

Noah went in, and his sons, and his wife, and his sons' wives with him, into the ark, because of the waters of the flood. There went in two and two unto Noah into the ark, the male and the female, as God had commanded Noah. In the six hundredth year of Noah's life, in the second month, the seventeenth day of the month, the same day were all the fountains of the great deep broken up, and the windows of heaven were opened . . . And every living substance was destroyed which was upon the face of the ground, both man, and cattle, and the creeping things, and the fowl of the heaven; and they were destroyed from the earth: and Noah only remained alive, and they that were with him in the ark.

The story of the flood in which all but a handful of the human race were wiped from the face of the Earth is one of the most compelling of the episodes in the Christian Bible. The idea that at some point in the distant past our ancestors passed through an apocalyptic era in which millions perished and the face of the Earth was changed for ever, seems to be deeply embedded in cultures all around the world.

The ancient Greeks had a tradition of the "supreme year", a period of thousands of years at the end of which the sun, moon and planets were reset in their original positions to the accompaniment of global cataclysms. The word "cataclysm", meaning a violent upheaval, comes from the Greek word *kataklysmos*, which was the term for the violent deluge at the end of the "supreme year". Heraclitus, a sixth-century BC Greek philosopher, taught that the deluge and rebirth takes place every 10,800 years. Aristarchus believed that the cycle took only 2,484 years. Two well-known Greek myths deal directly with apocalyptic events. The legend of Deucalion records a time when the whole world was covered with a flood that only Deucalion and his wife survived. The tale of Phaeton tells how the whole Earth was scorched in a terrible conflagration when a foolish man stole the chariot in which the sun rode across the sky and drove it too close to the ground.

Belief in a periodic apocalypse was by no means restricted to the Mediterranean region. The sacred Hindu text *Bhagavata Purana* teaches that mankind is living in the fifth age of the universe, each preceding age having been wiped out by a global cataclysm or *pralaya*. References to periodic world catastrophes are also found in the sacred books of the ancient Persian religion Mazdaism. One of the books of the *Avesta* counts seven ages punctuated by complete destruction. Chinese tradition also speaks of a "great year" that begins and ends with the destruction of the world. They named these past ages *kis* and count ten since the beginning of time. At the end of each *kis*:

> . . . *in a general convulsion of nature, the sea rises out of its bed, mountains are carried out of the ground, rivers are diverted from their courses, human beings and everything are ruined, and all traces of the ancients are erased.*

On the South American continent a similar belief was just as prevalent among the ancient inhabitants. The Incas, Aztecs and Mayans were all obsessed with compiling calendars and all recorded their belief that the world had passed through several ages that had ended in disaster. Polynesians, Hawaiians and Icelanders recognized nine previous ages of the Earth, each one going down in the blaze of a global firestorm, beneath a worldwide flood or the total destruction of an earthquake. In Jewish tradition the world is said to have passed through seven ages, each one a kind of trial run by the creator. These seven ages are said to have been punctuated by "abyss, chaos and water". Scholars have pointed out that the seven ages of Jewish myth are strongly echoed in the seven days and nights that the God of the Christian Old Testament took to create the Earth as it is today.

In 1950 the author Immanuel Velikovsky created a sensation with the publication of *Worlds in Collision*. He had long been fascinated by similarities in legends of global upheaval found in virtually every ancient culture, and speculated that these were actually memories of real, global events that had taken place within recorded history. Velikovsky believed that the orbits of the planets, particularly Venus, had changed radically over the past few thousand years and that these changes had created such extreme gravitational disruption in the Earth that tremendous hurricanes, firestorms and earthquakes had wrought almost total destruction on the peoples of the Earth. Many of his theories were based on events in the Old Testament, such as the story of Joshua who prayed that the sun and moon should be stopped in the sky. Velikovsky saw this as evidence that the Earth's orbit was under-going a radical shift as another, massive heavenly body passed close by.

Advances in scientific knowledge since Velikovsky wrote his ground-breaking and thought-provoking book have largely discredited the specifics of his theories, but the underlying insight – that global catastrophes may have taken place during the brief existence of *Homo sapiens* – remains a powerful one. In recent years we have become much more aware of the possibility that an event totally beyond our control could destroy civilization. During the hundreds of years in which European civilization was dominated by the beliefs and values of the Christian church, it was believed that the world was under the direction of God and was not subject to random calamities from outside. Few people are quite so sure today.

In 1995 an article appeared in *Science* magazine which provided powerful scientific evidence that the human race had been subject to a near apocalyptic catastrophe sometime within the past 400,000 years. Scientists studying variations in the genetic make-up of racial and cultural groups around the world made some startling discoveries. According to our current understanding of evolution, the genome for any particular species is constantly subject to tiny, random variations or mutations caused by errors in the copying of genetic information from generation to generation. It is the accumulation of these tiny variations over periods of time measured in millions of years that allows species to evolve. The older a species is the more genetic variations will accumulate. What surprised the geneticists was the remarkable uniformity of human DNA – there turned out to be far fewer mutations on average across the global population than they had expected to find.

The concept of genetic variation can be very misleading. To a non-scientist the very considerable differences in physical appearance between, say, a Kalahari bushman and an Inuit Eskimo, would seem to indicate a great deal of genetic difference. In fact this is not the case; genetically they are more than 99.9 per cent identical – appearance really is only skin deep. The study found that any two gorillas living in the same forest in central Africa are likely to have a greater degree of genetic difference than any two human beings living anywhere on the planet. This is puzzling because gorillas and humans have been around for roughly the same amount of time, so the scientists expected them to have roughly the same number of genetic variations. In fact they found so few variations in human DNA that it looks like the human gene pool began around 400,000 years ago. This leads to a startling conclusion – at some point the worldwide human population was reduced to such a tiny number that almost all mutations that had occurred in the millions of years before that point were wiped clean. Geneticists who conducted the study estimate that the global population may have been reduced to as few as 10,000 fertile individuals.

This massive crash from an estimated global population of several million to about the number of people in a small town, forced *Homo sapiens* through a bottleneck that effectively meant that the species began anew. This was our Adam and Eve generation, a tiny beleaguered population on the edge of extinction from whom we have inherited our genetic make-up. What genetics cannot tell us is why this crash happened, or how quickly. It may have taken a thousand years for the population to fail so spectacularly, or it may have taken forty days and forty nights as the story of Noah tells us. Given the evidence for a worldwide apocalypse myth it's tempting to attribute the near annihilation of the human race to a natural catastrophe – an event so terrible that the echo of its memory has been passed down over the millennia to our own time.

There is no shortage of suspects to fit the role of global killer. Asteroid collision is a very real threat and has been very much in vogue recently. A mass of dense rock a few kilometres in diameter impacting on the Earth's surface would cause a fireball more vast and powerful than all the world's thermonuclear weapons exploding at once. Giant tidal waves several kilometres high would sweep the continents and anything that survived would be slowly suffocated under a pall of ash and smoke that could block out the sun for decades. Disease is another very real possibility. The Black Death of the fourteenth century mercilessly wiped out a third of the population of Europe; if it had been an airborne variety, instead of relying on flea bites for its transmission, it's hard to imagine that any more than a tiny percentage would have survived. Perturbations in the Earth's orbit caused by a close encounter with a massive heavenly body or unexpected, violent solar activity could also cause global catastrophes. Whatever it was that nearly killed us off we cannot preclude the possibility that it could happen again. If the ancients were right, who can say when this cycle will end?

The Doomed of Roanoke

Strangers in a strange land

On 18 August 1586 a child was born in the New England colony of Virginia – the first European colony in North America. She was the first child of European descent to be born on the newly discovered continent and was appropriately christened "Virginia". Her grandfather was John White, an agent of Sir Walter Raleigh, who left her, her parents and 117 other brave souls to establish a permanent colony where a previous expedition two years before had failed. For Virginia and the others the future was far from certain. Today America is regarded as the land of opportunity, but 300 years ago it was an unexplored and dangerous place described by Queen Elizabeth I as "remote, heathen and barbarous". Little Virginia Dare's fate was to be stranger and more terrible than anyone imagined.

Much of the detailed exploration of the coast of North America was carried out by Sir Walter Raleigh's stepbrother, Humphrey Gilbert. It was Gilbert who claimed Newfoundland in the name of Queen Elizabeth I in 1583, a voyage that cost him his life when his ship met severe storms on the return journey. Gilbert had always meant to establish a permanent English colony in the New World and this task now fell to Raleigh. Permission was obtained from the queen in

March 1584 in a document that demanded that one fifth of any recovered treasure must go to the crown. Two ships, captained by Philip Amadas and Arthur Barlowe, set sail the following month and made good progress across the Atlantic via the Canary Islands. On reaching the American continent the expedition proceeded northwards and eventually put in to a sheltered cove 125 miles up from the Florida coast. The area was explored and turned out to be an island rather than part of the mainland. It was named Virginia in honour of Elizabeth I who was known as the Virgin Queen (the island is now called Roanoke Island). Game was plentiful and the land extremely fertile. A tribe of natives living on the island proved to be surprisingly welcoming and their leader, Granganimeo, became friendly with the leaders of the expedition. By September the explorers were back in England full of nothing but praise and enthusiasm for the wonders of Virginia.

By the following spring a fleet of seven ships, under the command of Sir Richard Grenville, was putting ashore a group of a hundred men to found a permanent colony on Roanoke Island. The following year Sir Francis Drake, who had been in the West Indies raiding Spanish treasure ships, decided to call in at the colony with his fleet of twenty-three ships. The colonists, at least those who had survived, were overjoyed to see them. Things had not gone well. The colonists were unable to grow their own food and had had to rely on the local tribes for support. The friendly Granganimeo had died and been replaced by his son Pemisapan who had taken a dislike to the colony and tried to destroy it. Other tribes on the island had also joined in the fray. Many colonists died in the fighting and many others had succumbed to starvation and disease during the harsh winter. Drake agreed to evacuate the colonists, but before they could leave for England, his fleet was hit by a storm and fifteen men had to be left behind. None of them were ever seen again.

Despite the disasters that had befallen the first colony, Raleigh sent a second expedition the following year. Surviving members of the first colony had reported large deposits of copper ore on the island and rich pearl beds along the coast, and Raleigh was determined to take advantage of these possibilities to further his political career. It was this second expedition under John White that left the 120 men and women on Roanoke Island in the summer of 1586, among them young Virginia.

White sailed for England before the coming winter made the Atlantic crossing too hazardous, promising to return the following year. Unfortunately international politics was to make this impossible. Rivalry over exploitation of the New World and religious differences meant that a virtual state of war had existed between England and Spain for several years. On the open seas English ships routinely plundered Spanish gold galleons returning from South America and Spanish ships responded in kind when the opportunity arose. All-out war was coming and in the spring of 1587, before White could set out for Roanoke, the English government stopped vessels from leaving English ports. The following year, now desperate to return to Virginia, White managed to persuade two captains to ignore the ban and set out for America. They had not got far when a hostile encounter with a French vessel forced them to return. War finally came later that year in the form of the Spanish Armada, a mighty floating army that looked set to sweep the English Navy from the seas and Queen Elizabeth from her throne. Stormy weather and the skill of Sir Francis Drake's defence thwarted the Armada, but it was too late for an expedition that year. In the meantime Raleigh had lost interest in Virginia and turned his attention to acquiring wealth in Ireland. The Roanoke colonists had now been totally alone for three years.

Finally in the spring of 1590 White managed to get an expedition together. He arrived in the New World with three vessels in August of that year, only to be met with an eerie silence. Not a soul responded to their hails and when they reached the settlement they found it completely deserted. The primitive homesteads had been replaced by a sturdy wooden palisade which was broken and burned in places. Huts inside the compound had been ransacked and no sign of the colonists' belongings remained. There were several new graves. Searches of the surrounding area were carried out but revealed nothing. Then somebody noticed a word carved into one of the corner posts of the palisade. It simply read "Croatoan". White thought this might be the name of a tribal village about fifty miles away, but could not be sure.

The rapidly worsening weather and the nervousness of his crews who had no wish to stay in such an eerie place forced White to abandon the search. He was unable to find anyone to finance another expedition and the fate of the colonists was never discovered. White never knew what became of his granddaughter but was forced to accept that she must be dead along with all of the others.

Eventually, permanent colonies were established in

North America and most of the continent's native peoples suffered the same fate that everyone believed had befallen the Roanoke colonists – massacre or starvation. Occasionally colonists came across tribes of Indians who were not surprised at the strange appearance of white people. They spoke of a tribe of blue-eyed or fair-skinned people who had lived in the area now known as Virginia in the time of their fathers or grandfathers. Most people who had never heard of Roanoke dismissed these stories as legend but for some it raised a chilling possibility. What if the Roanoke colonists had not perished but simply fled the island to find a safer haven? Perhaps the mysterious word "Croatoan" had been a message that was simply not understood.

One can only imagine the hardship faced by these people. Cut off from everything they knew by thousands of miles of ocean they were alone in a harsh and threatening world, they might as well have been marooned on a distant planet. Year after year they endured the bitter winters wondering why White never returned. Finally forced to leave even the rudimentary civilization of their homesteads they wandered into the forests of the mainland and were eventually swallowed up by the vast continent. What of young Virginia? Perhaps she too survived and, unencumbered by memories of home, thrived in the New World, a stranger in a strange land.

An interesting footnote to this story came almost three hundred years later in the 1980s when a team of archaeologists located and excavated the site of the lost colony of Roanoke Island. They found evidence of fires and primitive weapons that certainly indicated a number of violent struggles at the site. They also found bodies, some showing signs of violent death, others of fatal disease. However, they did not find nearly enough bodies to account for all of the colonists, and they did not find the body of a three-year-old girl who may have been named "Virginia".

The Hole in Symmes's Head

● ●

What NASA never told you

John Cleves Symmes was a man with an idea, an idea as strange and revolutionary as the one that had driven Christopher Columbus to try to reach the East by sailing west. Symmes believed with a dogged passion that the Earth was hollow. The strength of his conviction was to convert many of his contemporaries and to create weird ripples of belief that continued well into the twentieth century.

Between 1802 and 1816 John Symmes served in the United States Infantry, rising to the rank of captain for his dedication to duty and his bravery during the war of 1812. But there were other things on Symmes's mind. When he retired from the military in 1816 he settled in what was then the frontier town of St Louis. He took out the science and philosophy books that had fascinated him in his youth, and set up his telescope to study the universe. Inspired by ideas he found in the works of the great astronomer Halley, Symmes began to formulate his startling theory. In 1818 he felt ready to reveal these incredible conclusions to the world in his first publication, entitled *Circular No.1*. Along with the circular came a challenge.

TO ALL THE WORLD!

*I declare the earth is hollow, and habitable within;
containing a number of solid concentrick spheres,
one within the other, and that it is open at the poles
12 or 16 degrees; I pledge my life in support of this
truth, and am ready to explore the hollow, if the
world will support and aid me in the undertaking.*

*John Cleves Symmes
Of Ohio, late Captain of Infantry*

N.B.
*I ask one hundred brave companions, well
equipped, to start from Siberia in the fall season,
with reindeer and slays, on the ice of the frozen sea;
I engage we find warm and rich land, stocked with
thrifty vegetables and animals if not men, on
reaching one degree northward of latitude 82; we
will return in the succeeding spring.*
J. C. S

The circular cased a sensation, but not quite of the
kind Symmes had hoped for; of the numerous scientific and learned institutions worldwide to whom
Symmes had sent his circular few even bothered to
acknowledge receipt. Newspapers and news agencies,
however, leapt on Symmes's bizarre challenge with
relish and ridiculed him mercilessly for years to come.
What had possessed this sensible, correct military man
to make such incredible claims?

Symmes's vision was startling in its boldness. He
proposed that the Earth was essentially a hollow
sphere with a crust about 1000 miles thick. At the
North and South Poles, neither of which regions had
been explored in Symmes's time, he envisaged two

gaping holes that provided access to the interior of the sphere. These openings were vast – between 4000 and 6000 miles in diameter – and sloped so that a vessel crossing their rim would be unaware that they were heading "downward" for several hundred miles. Symmes contested that although explorers had been over the rims of these holes they had not gone far enough to realize it. Indeed, according to Symmes, known and explored areas of land, including Tierra del Fuego and New Zealand in the south and Alaska, Siberia and Greenland in the north, actually lay beyond the verge of the polar openings. He believed that the Magellanic Clouds, two bright nebulae visible from the southern hemisphere, were in fact the images of Tasmania and New Zealand seen across the southern polar opening. Within the hollow Earth Symmes's theory saw a series of progressively smaller spheres, themselves open at the poles.

For Symmes the most compelling evidence for his theory was the failure of explorers successfully to navigate the polar regions or to reach the poles themselves. He believed that the entire rims of both polar openings were magnetized and that explorers who believed they were approaching the poles were just wandering around the rim plateaux. He was convinced that an expedition led by him, and armed with a true understanding of the nature of the Earth, would succeed in reaching the interior regions. Although dismissed by scientists and ridiculed by the press, there were some who found Symmes's pamphlets and lectures compelling. Many of these converts would point to the fact that had it not been for the similarly ridiculed exploits of Christopher Columbus, their own country would never have come into existence. Several motions were put before the American Congress by members of the House of Representatives urging that the United States should mount a major polar expedition with Symmes at its head. The goal of this expedition would be to reach the interior regions of the Earth and establish trade with its inhabitants. Symmes was bitterly disappointed when the government he had served so well refused to fund him. Who knows what such an expedition, driven by the American pioneering spirit and Symmes's indomitable perseverance, would have achieved?

After years of lecturing and writing Symmes came no closer to his goal until, in 1825, the Russian government granted him permission to join an expedition into Siberia. It seemed that at last he would have revenge on his critics but, at the last moment, he had to pull out through lack of money and the Russian expedition went ahead without his guidance. Symmes never came so close to achieving his goal again and he died in 1829 at the age of forty-nine. His idea, however, didn't die with him.

In 1871 a thick volume entitled *The Hollow Globe* was published in Chicago. Its authors, Dr M. L. Sherman in collaboration with Professor Lyon and a host of spirits from the afterlife, presented their revelations that the Earth is a hollow sphere to a less than enthusiastic world. *The Hollow Globe* predicted that a passage to the interior would be found in time for the centenary of the Declaration of Independence and that it was the destiny of the United States to exploit the lands that would be found within. In 1906 another book appeared that took Symmes's idea into the twentieth century and gave it a new lease of life. *The Phantom of the Poles* by William Reed is perhaps the most elegant exposition of the hollow Earth theory to come out of the grand tradition of the nineteenth-century amateur theorist.

Reed based *The Phantom of the Poles* on his exhaustive study of the polar expeditions of the nineteenth century. Like Symmes he became convinced that the poles had never been reached because they were not there – his book was published three years before Robert Peary finally reached the North Pole. He pointed to a number of perplexing phenomena that had been observed by these expeditions to add weight to his argument. Why, he asked, is there snow apparently coloured by plant pollen in the polar regions; why are icebergs frequently filled with rocks and gravel, what is the aurora borealis and why do meteors frequently fall near the poles? Reed believed that the answers to all these questions was the presence of polar doorways that opened on to a vast interior world of lush vegetation, mineral wealth, seas and volcanic activity. Reed, like many hollow earthers before him, envisaged the Earth's interior as a kind of ready-made paradise where men would be able to enjoy a perfect climate, plentiful resources and create the ideal society. In many ways the visions of these men were a yearning for the days when their own country was a vast and unexplored paradise waiting to be made into the perfect society – a dream that had not been realized to anyone's satisfaction.

In 1913, four years after explorers had actually reached the North Pole, a vibrant new voice proclaimed the hollow Earth hypothesis once again. *A Journey to the Earth's Interior* by Marshall B. Gardner was heavily inspired by Symmes's and Reed's ideas, although its author scorned both men as fools whose theories were far too simple to have captured the truth. According to Gardner the Earth was not just hollow but contained a second sun, about six hundred miles in diameter, which provided a source of heat and light for the inhabitants of the inner world. The polar phenomena known as the aurora borealis were clear evidence to Gardner that this internal sun existed, since they could only be created by its rays shinning through the polar openings. As further proof Gardner pointed to the recently discovered astronomical phenomena known as nebulae. According to modern astronomers these are vast, expanding shells of gases surrounding the remnants of an exploded star. For Gardner these were clearly other worlds like the Earth in the process of formation – he saw a bright central sun and a shell of material condensing around it to form a hollow planet.

Another oddity that excited Gardner was the occasional discovery of complete mammoth bodies frozen in the polar ice. Palaeontologists speculated that these corpses were more than ten thousand years old and had been preserved by the extreme cold. According to Gardner this was absurd – the mammoth clearly survived, along with many other species thought to be extinct, on the wide lush plains of the Earth's interior. As with other proponents of the hollow Earth theory Gardner's dream was of vast new realms waiting to be exploited by the benevolent and wise American race. In the second edition of *The Phantom of the Poles* Gardner makes a stirring prediction.

> *For this discovery would add the most glorious page yet written to the annals of the United States. Once we have made this discovery in actual*

*physical fact – as it is already made in reason and
thought – feeding Europe would be mere bagatelle.
We could feed the world and have an unlimited
plenty left over. We could not only feed the world
but we could transform the world. A new and
glorious chapter in the history of the human race
would have opened.*

As noble and humanitarian as Gardner's vision no
doubt was, it rings certain alarm bells in the modern
mind. Another movement that believed its destiny was
to "open a glorious new chapter in the history of the
human race" was just beginning to take root in post-
World War I Germany as Gardner wrote these words.
Among the many ideas and theories that went into the
bizarre melting pot of Nazi philosophy was the old
hollow Earth theory in a new and extreme form.

Peter Bender was one of the daring young men who
fought in the world's first air war. He was a German pilot
in World War I. Shot down over France in 1917 Bender
spent a year in a POW camp recovering from terrible
wounds. It was here that he came across the hollow
Earth theory in old magazine articles. Bender's vision,
formed after years of study and contemplation during
the inter-war years, essentially turned Symmes's
original concept on its head. According to Bender, the
Earth is indeed a hollow sphere surrounding a central
sun, but we live on the inside of the sphere not the
outside. Bender was aware that his vision was
completely at variance with every belief of science and
common sense – perhaps that is what convinced him.
He devised elegant and complex explanations for why
the world appeared to be so different from what he
knew it to be. In the ordinary course of events Bender

probably would have died an obscure eccentric to whom nobody paid any attention, but these were no ordinary times. For one thing, one of Bender's flying comrades had been Hermann Göring, the man who was to become Reichsmarschal of Nazi Germany and one of Hitler's most trusted commanders.

The Nazis had a tremendous weakness for occult theories and theorists – especially those that allowed them to justify their vision of an Aryan master race destined to rule the world. Bender's theory, among others, were seen as proof that Aryan science could reveal the truth, while mainstream science, dominated by Jews like Einstein, was a mere illusion meant to hide it. In 1933 an engineer named Mengering became convinced by Bender's theory and proposed a project to prove it. Mengering's idea was to launch a manned rocket directly into the sky so that it would eventually reach the far side of the hollow globe and land in New Zealand. Amazingly Mengering got the funding he needed and construction began. Fortunately the plan was revised and there was no pilot when Mengering's rocket slewed wildly off its launch pad and crashed into the ground 300 metres away.

In 1942, at the height of the World War II, another project based on Bender's theory got under way. Someone at the German Naval Research Institute realized that if the surface of the Earth was indeed concave and not convex as everyone assumed, then it would be possible to locate enemy ships in the North Sea or Atlantic simply by pointing a camera into the sky at the correct angle. According to Bender, the illusion of a convex Earth was caused by the upper atmosphere severely refracting light in the visible wavelengths. To get around this problem special infrared cameras were constructed – since it was believed that infrared light would not be refracted nearly as much. An experimental station was set up on Rügen Island in the Baltic and hundreds of photographs were taken with the camera pointed at forty-five degrees into the sky. Not surprisingly no enemy warships were captured on film. Shortly afterwards Bender, his wife and his closest supporters were sent to a Nazi death camp. A failed theorist was a dangerous thing to be in Germany in 1942.

Despite all official records stating that the Rügen Island experiment was a failure, and despite the numerous successful expeditions to the poles undertaken in the twentieth century, there are those who continue to be beguiled by the vision of Symmes's hollow Earth. A popular modern theory holds that Nazi scientists did indeed discover an entrance to an inner world at the poles and that Hitler, with the remnants of his regime, retired there when defeat became inevitable. According to the adherents of this Nazi survival theory, Hitler is still there today and the strange craft that are sometimes mistaken for extra-terrestrial visitors are actually his advanced scout planes watching for the moment to return and continue the war. The twentieth century's greatest occultist, Helena Blavatsky, taught that the fate of the Earth was watched over by a group of superhuman beings known as the Secret Masters. Originally these wise guardians were said to live in a vast underground city in Tibet known as Shambhala. Later Blavatsky and others identified Shambhala with the hollow world that had all begun in the head of John Cleves Symmes.

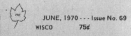

FLYING SAUCERS

JUNE, 1970 - - - Issue No. 69
WISCO   75¢

MYSTERIES OF THE SPACE AGE

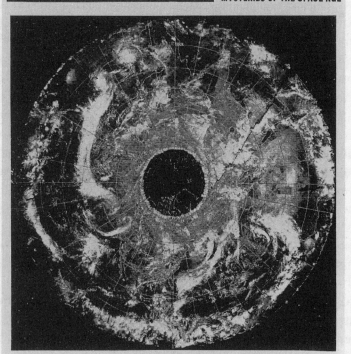

FIRST PHOTOS OF THE HOLE AT THE POLE !
Satellites ESSA - 3 and ESSA -7 Penetrate Cloud Cover!
Mariners Also Photograph Martian Polar Opening!

Satellite photo supposedly showing a vast opening at the
North Pole. In fact the dark disc is the area of the pole in
perpetual winter darkness.

The Aeronauts
••••••••••••••••••••••••••••••

The original ufonauts?

We are familiar today with tales of strange craft seen in the skies but few people realize that cases of unidentified flying objects were being regularly reported more than 120 years ago. From 1880 there was a spate of sightings of huge craft known as airships. The sightings began in the United States and, over the next thirty years, spread to Europe and even New Zealand. The origin of these huge, dirigible-type craft has never been discovered. Whoever or whatever created them had developed a technology at least fifty years ahead of the time. Although hot-air balloons had been built since the eighteenth century, the notion of using lighter-than-air gases, such as helium or hydrogen, in conjunction with a powerful engine to create a heavier-than-air craft was still a theory in 1880. It wasn't until 1903 that Orville Wright made the first recognized, controlled flight in a heavier-than-air craft (he covered 36.5 metres, less than the wingspan of a modern Boeing 747).

On the night of 26 March 1880, the station master of the small town of Galistoe Junction, New Mexico (the town is now called Lamy), was taking a short walk with two friends when he noticed the sound of voices that seemed to be coming from the air. Puzzled, the three men looked around and then spotted an incredible sight. They saw a vast, fish-shaped object sailing in from the west. It was flying slowly and was low enough for the men to make out strange symbols painted on its sides. They could see windows and people moving about inside. As the craft came closer, strange music could be heard emanating from inside, and the sound of voices speaking an unfamiliar language. The witnesses later reported that it sounded like a society cocktail party was slowly drifting over their heads. As the vessel passed, a few of its occupants could be seen leaning over the side of a kind of walkway, pointing and gesticulating at the three men on the ground; they also dropped objects which the men hurried to find in the gathering gloom.

The next day, two of the strange gifts dropped by the airship were put on display in the railway depot. One was a curious and beautiful flower with a strip of ribbon attached. Painted on the ribbon were characters which everyone agreed looked like the Chinese script they had seen on crates of tea. The other object was a delicate cup described by the *Santa Fe Daily New Mexican* as "entirely different from anything used in this country". Later that day a man said to be of "Asian appearance" arrived in the town and offered a large sum of money for the artefacts, which he said were of ancient origin. One report claims that a wealthy Chinaman, who visited the area a week later, met the purchaser of the airship artefacts and grew extremely excited, saying that here was proof that Chinese experiments in flying had finally succeeded. By the end of the decade airships had been seen in nineteen American states.

The public was already very familiar with the concept of airships. Since the 1840s various plans had been put forward for their construction and many inventors had worked on perfecting such a machine. In 1848, when gold fever hit California, a company based in New York promised a cheap reliable air service for those who wanted to seek their fortune. A pamphlet advertising the service featured a huge airship with an enclosed passenger car underneath for up to fifty people; propulsion was to be provided by a long pipe spewing superheated steam. The pamphlet promised: "It is expected to put this machine in operation about the first of April 1849, and the transport is expected to make a trip to the gold region and back in seven days . . ." Even leaving aside the rather suspicious date of the proposed launch, this was probably simply a joke or a scam designed to con those desperate to get to the gold fields. However, it shows that the idea of travelling in an airship was largely accepted, and it wasn't too much of a wild leap of the imagination to envisage flying cross-country within a year. Other airship projects were taken rather more seriously.

In the same year, a young German named Dellschau emigrated to the United States. He took up residence in the town of Sonora, California, where he founded a mysterious and cult-like society known as the Aero Club. Details of this secret, underground organization dedicated to the construction of flying machines only emerged in 1969 when a UFO researcher unearthed a number of Dellschau's bizarre notebooks. The volumes describe a number of flying devices which Dellschau claimed all flew from a secret airbase in the mountains. The books also reveal that the Aero Club was just a part of a much larger and decidedly sinister organization referred to as NYMZA. It appears that the engineers of the Aero Club were exclusively members of staff of a test facility run by an international organization totally outside the control of governments. Whether the NYMZA ever existed or was just a figment of Dellschau's rather vivid imagination is impossible to say. It is recorded, however, that one member of the Aero Club was killed in a mid-air explosion after he threatened to share his knowledge with the outside world.

Among Dellschau's notes were drawings of the craft reputedly flown by the Aero Club, and these are less than convincing at first sight. Most are winged contraptions suspended under gas bags, but the volume of the gas bags seems far too small to have supported their weight. References are made, however, to a type of experimental gas called NB which, apparently, negated the effects of gravity and allowed the machines to ascend. It's tempting to imagine a dedicated group of aeronauts solving the problems of heavier-than-air transport in a remote field in the California mountains. After all, the Wright brothers were no different, and there are half-confirmed cases of other engineers achieving startling breakthroughs even before them. In 1895, Bill Frost, a Welshman from Cardigan Bay, was said to have flown a vertical take-off aircraft for several minutes over the fields of Stammers Hill. The *Guinness Book of Records* recognizes Henri Giffard of Paris as the first airship flier; his forty-four metre-long coal-gas inflated craft took to the air in September 1852.

The greatest number of mystery airship sightings took place in the years 1896 and 1897. On 17 November 1896 the *Sacramento Bee* printed a telegram it had received from a New York man, which claimed that he and his friends would fly an airship of their own invention over the town on their way to California. The very next day the paper printed a sensational article.

> *People standing on the sidewalks at certain points in the city between the hours stated [six and seven o'clock], saw coming through the air over the housetops, what appeared to them to be merely an electric arc lamp propelled by some mysterious force.*
>
> *It came out of the east and sailed unevenly towards the south-west, dropping now nearer to the earth, and now suddenly rising into the air again as if the force that was whirling it through space was sensible of the dangers of collision with the objects on the earth.*
>
> *Hundreds of persons saw it. Those who got the closest look said the object was huge and cigar-shaped and had four large wings attached to an aluminium body. Some insisted they heard voices and raucous laughter emanating from the ship.*

In the nights that followed, dozens of other witnesses reported seeing the Sacramento airship as it made its way across the Southwest. In November of the same year a man calling himself E. H. Benjamin appeared in the office of a San Francisco lawyer and asked for legal help to patent an airship. Benjamin claimed that he was the representative of the man who had flown the vessel over Sacramento and that the inventor was now ready to reveal the secrets of his machine to the world. Apparently the inventor changed his mind because no such patent application was made.

The following year the sightings continued. On 15

April the story took a new twist when an airship sighted over the town of Appleton, Wisconsin, apparently dropped a message to witnesses on the ground. The *Grand Rapids Evening Press* reprinted its contents the following day.

> *Aboard the airship* Pegasus, *April 9th 1897.*
> *The problem of aerial navigation has been solved. The writers have spent the past month cruising about in the airship* Pegasus *and have demonstrated to their complete satisfaction that the ship is a thorough success. We have been able to obtain a speed of 150 miles an hour and have risen to a height of 2,500 feet above sea level . . . Within a month our application for the patents for a parallel plane airship will be filed simultaneously at Washington and the European capitals. The ship is propelled by steam and is lighted by electricity, and has a carrying power of 1,000 pounds.*

Once again the promised patents never emerged. Neither was there any explanation for why the aeronauts chose such an indirect method of communicating their success to the press. Perhaps the *Pegasus*'s voyage ended in disaster, a possibility raised by another note from the sky which was found tied to a bottle opener on the ground in Grand Rapids.

> *To whoever finds this:*
> *We are 2,500 feet above the level of the sea, headed north at this writing, testing the airship. Afraid we are lost. We are unable to control our engine. Please notify our people. Think we are somewhere over Michigan.*

Arthur B. Coats, Laurel, Mississippi
C.C. Harris, Gulfport, Mississippi
C.W. Rich, Richburg, Mississippi

By 1909 the great airship mystery had migrated across the Atlantic to Britain. The first sighting was on 25 March in Peterborough. The witness, PC Kettle, was patrolling the town when he heard the sound of what he assumed was a motor car engine. Hoping to catch sight of the vehicle, a rare sight in 1909, Kettle was perplexed to find that the sound was getting louder but that there was no motor car in sight. Finally he realized that the throbbing, buzzing noise was coming from overhead and looked up to see a blinding light shining down at him. The searchlight swept across the ground and the bemused policeman could see that it was attached to a craft so huge and low that it blocked out the stars over the street. He watched in astonishment as the vessel accelerated away to the south. As he had expected, his report prompted no more than a recommendation that he take several weeks' leave.

As in the United States, sightings began flooding in from all over the country. On the night of 13 May two men walking across Ham Common in London had a particularly fascinating encounter. They noticed a huge, cigar-shaped craft, which they later estimated to be at least 250 feet long, hovering just above the trees. As they cautiously approached to investigate, a powerful searchlight suddenly illuminated and picked them out. The craft descended until a gondola-like arrangement, slung under the main body of the airship, touched the ground. Two men got out and approached the terrified witnesses cordially. One, who spoke with an American accent, simply greeted them and commented on the mildness of the evening. The other, who had a German accent, asked for some tobacco for his pipe. Their short conversation over, the two aeronauts returned to their craft and ascended into the night sky. Both witnesses commented that the airship headed in a northerly direction at an incredible speed which they estimated to be in excess of eighty miles an hour. Airships were being built in Germany and France at the time of the Ham Common encounter but nothing that could have easily made the journey there, and certainly nothing that was capable of reaching eighty miles an hour.

Shortly after the 1909 airship mystery began, the German government announced that it was planning to begin a scheduled airship service that could encompass the whole of Europe and beyond. This came as a shock to the British who were suddenly faced with the prospect of Germany dominating the skies of Europe. The proposed German airships were to be 250 feet long and capable of speeds up to eighty miles an hour, an exact match for the Ham Common vessel. Could it be that German airships had been ready for some time, ranging across the empty skies of Europe at will, perhaps even dropping in on Ham Common to stock up on pipe tobacco? It seems possible. The German inventor Graf von Zeppelin built his first prototype airship in 1900 and by 1910 he was known to be building models capable of thirty-five miles per hour. The speed of objects in the air is very hard to judge, especially at night, and the Ham Common witnesses had probably never seen anything in their life that travelled at eighty miles an hour. It raises the intriguingly romantic image of aerial explorers wandering the globe, oblivious to international

The Graf Zeppelin II was the largest airship ever flown. It weighed 210 tons and measured 245 metres. Her maiden flight took place on 14 September 1938.

borders and totally alone in a sky where aircraft were still virtually unknown.

A few years later, during World War I, the Germans demonstrated their superior aerial technology by placing a fleet of Zeppelins over Norfolk and dropping bombs on the defenceless towns below. In May 1915, eleven Zeppelins carried out the first of twelve bombing raids on London. By the end of the war Britain had been hit by more than fifty airship raids.

These raids contributed very little to the German war effort and caused minimal damage to their targets, but they clearly demonstrate that if airships were capable of making the trip from Germany to Britain in 1915 there is no reason to believe that they couldn't have done it six years earlier. As to the US sightings ten years earlier, it is well known that Europeans of many nationalities emigrated to America in the latter half of the nineteenth century, and that among them were many scientists and inventors hoping to find the opportunity to pursue projects that their own conservative governments had no interest in. It's not difficult to conceive of a lone inventor achieving a breakthrough comparable to that of the Wright brothers a few years later. Perhaps one day we will discover who he was and how he did it.

Mad Science

●●●●●●●●●●●●●●●●●●●●●●●●●●●●●●●●●●

Frankenstein's forgotten brothers

Science has given us almost everything. The slow and agonizing process by which we have gained an understanding of the laws of nature and, by extension, the means to turn them to our own ends, has delivered us from the brutal world of our ancestors. A thousand years ago humanity was almost totally at the mercy of disease, starvation and the elements. Today there are very few natural forces, apart from extreme storms and earthquakes, that can threaten our comfortable daily existence. The fact that a large proportion of the world's population lives without these benefits is a political and social failing rather than a failing of science.

Despite these incredible advantages the scientist has long been the focus of mystery and suspicion. Mary Shelley's classic novel *Frankenstein* has come to define our fears and suspicions about scientists, but the roots of the problem go back even further. Humans are innately superstitious; we readily imagine unseen forces at work in the natural world around us. The scientist plays the dangerous game of disregarding some of our most basic fears and instincts and arousing our suspicions in the process. There is a basic fear that the scientist is meddling with things that are not meant to be understood by humans, that he or she is "playing God". In *Frankenstein* the fear is manifested by the evil nature of the creature that the scientist creates – science allows him to create life, but not to give it a moral sense or purpose.

The image of the mad scientist toying with terrible powers in his gothic laboratory is a persistent and powerful one. Even today the suspicion that the men in white coats are doing things that no sane or right-thinking person would want to meddle with surfaces in regular newspaper scares about nuclear power, space death-rays or genetic engineering. The truth is of course that scientists are just as moral and ordinary as the rest of us – for the most part. There is, however, a long tradition of lone inventors who have toiled in secret over their extraordinary creations, making discoveries and constructing theories that remain poorly understood to this day. Many of these strange men, for they have been exclusively men, are characters straight out of a Hammer Horror gothic movie.

Nikola Tesla is perhaps the strangest and most disturbing of these hidden scientists, partly because he started his life as one of the greatest acknowledged geniuses of his age. Nikola Tesla was born in Serbo-Croatia in 1856. He studied at the Polytechnic School at Graz and at the University of Prague, where he became fascinated with electrical phenomena – a study then very much in its infancy. To the outrage of his teachers, Tesla insisted that he could build an entirely new kind of electric motor that would be far more efficient than the direct current, or DC, motors that existed at the time. Ignoring advice that such a device was impossible, he went ahead and built a prototype – the world's first alternating current, or AC, motor. Despite the obvious advantages of his motor,

Tesla could find no one in Europe who was interested in the project; he emigrated to the United States in 1884 where he got work with the famous American inventor Thomas Edison.

It's an extraordinary fact that, although Edison is remembered and revered in the West today, Tesla, whose inventions changed the world, is virtually unknown. Tesla's contributions to the field of electrical engineering cannot be overestimated. Virtually every electronic device in use today owes its existence to Tesla's AC system. It was Tesla who made the international network of electrical power grids that supply our homes, offices and factories possible. In the hands of George Westinghouse, Tesla's technological developments literally transformed the world. Among his many inventions was the Tesla coil, a kind of magnifying device for electrical voltage, that made televisions and computer monitors possible. It was while working on this device that he became interested in resonance – the way in which waves are multiplied in power by the addition of other waves. Resonance applies to waves of all kinds – from the sea to electromagnetic radiation such as radio waves.

Tesla wondered just how powerful he could make an electromagnetic wave. After a fire destroyed his lab in New York, Tesla moved to Colorado Springs where a friend had offered to supply him with as much free electricity as he needed for his experiments. Tesla knew that if you send an electric charge into the ground it passes right through the Earth and bounces back without losing a lot of energy. He figured that by reinforcing the wave at just the right frequency every time it bounced back, he could create an electrical flow more powerful than anything seen before. Between

Nikola Tesla memorial on Goat Island, Niagra Falls, Ontario, Canada

1898 and 1899 Tesla built a huge resonating coil and carried out endless experiments to get it in tune with the resonating frequency of the Earth. Finally, he was ready. The apparatus was switched on and Tesla retired outside to watch the results, wearing three-inch rubber insulated soles to be on the safe side.

On top of his lab Tesla had erected a 200-foot antenna to discharge current into the air as lightning. As the energy pulses surged back and forth through the Earth, traversing 6000 miles of rock and molten lava in about a thirtieth of a second, the resonance effect began to build up. Suddenly a six-foot arc of coruscating, artificial lightning burst from the tower. The rebounding waves quickly cranked the surges up to bolts twenty feet long, then fifty, then eighty feet. The surges were so powerful now that the whole area was lit up with an unearthly blue glow and each discharge was creating thunderclaps that could be heard twenty-two miles away. There seemed to be no limit to the power build-up as Tesla's artificial lightning bolts reached 120 feet. Then, suddenly everything went quiet. Tesla's experiment had burned out his friend's power station and blacked out every house in the area. It is fortunate that Tesla carried out his experiment in 1899; had it been today, every electrical device in a fifty-mile radius would have been utterly wrecked!

It was surely one of the most incredible experiments ever carried out and certainly one of the most spectacular. Tesla had used the entire planet as a resonator and generated magnitudes of power that would not be seen again until the advent of the atomic bomb forty-five years later. Almost a hundred years later, in the late 1980s, amateur radio enthusiasts began picking up strange electromagnetic interference. The source was tracked to two sites in the then Soviet Union and it was soon apparent that the Russians were experimenting with high power Tesla coils. There was a great deal of speculation about what the Soviets were up to, but the most rational explanation was that they were trying to develop a device that could knock out electronic equipment – such as missile guidance systems – on the other side of the world. This wasn't the first time that Tesla's work was put to use as a potential weapon of war. Tesla himself was said to be working on a death ray – an extreme range electromagnetic weapon – in the early years of the twentieth century.

Tesla claimed that he could build a weapon capable of knocking aircraft out of the sky thousands of miles away. It isn't known for certain whether he ever built such a machine, much less used it, but it would be unwise to dismiss the claims of a man who demonstrated time and again that he was capable of incredible feats of invention and innovation. Some researchers have connected Tesla's secret death ray weapon with the mysterious and powerful explosion that rocked the Tunguska region of Siberia one night in 1909. The Tunguska blast was more powerful than any thermonuclear detonation ever created by man. Most theories attribute it to a comet or meteor exploding in the upper atmosphere. Whatever caused the explosion it flattened thousands of square miles of forest and lit up the skies of western Europe with a false dawn that caused many to believe that the end of the world had come. No theory has satisfactorily explained the Tunguska event. Strange traces of radiation found in the area and the absence of an impact crater have led many to dismiss the comet-meteor theory and look for alternative explanations.

At the time of the explosion Robert Peary was making his second attempt to reach the North Pole, and Tesla had mysteriously announced that he would attempt to communicate with the expedition as it crossed the ice. He urged Peary to watch out for any strange phenomenon in the Arctic skies and report back exactly what he had seen. It has been suggested that Tesla intended to test his death ray by flashing it across the Arctic skies but that something went wrong and the ray struck the earth at Tunguska. Whatever the truth, no more was heard about Tesla's death ray, perhaps the great man decided to end the project when he realized he had come within a hair's breadth of taking out a major European city.

Other projects that Tesla was working on at the time promised a revolution as profound as the one he had wrought with the introduction of the AC power network. Back in New York he set about building a vast facility which he claimed would become the first stage in a worldwide network of receivers that would allow power to be transmitted instantaneously, and in any amount, to anywhere on the planet. The new project was funded by J. P. Morgan, then the wealthiest man in the United States, and was based at a laboratory Tesla had built on Long Island, named Wardenclyffe.

However, just as Tesla promised that concrete results were not far away, Morgan experienced financial difficulties and stopped supporting what could have been the greatest breakthrough of our age. By this stage Tesla was not just talking about the wireless transmission of power, he claimed he could extract unlimited power from the air. But his ideas were becoming too grandiose, even for those who had seen the success of his earlier work at first hand, and funding dried up almost completely. George Westinghouse and others had become extremely wealthy from Tesla's inventions, and they weren't about to fund a scheme that would give unlimited free power to everyone in the world, thereby bankrupting their own industry in the process.

Tesla lived until 1943 but he never again had the money to put his ideas into practice on a grand scale, and he increasingly came to be labelled as a crank by the media. In his later years he gave birthday press conferences which were attended by pressmen hungry for the latest crazy prediction from the country's favourite mad scientist. Although many of the ideas he talked about later became a reality, including radar,

microwave technology and beamed television transmission, they were presented as the ravings of a loony
old man. It is quite possible that Tesla had indeed lost
his grip on reality and that his claims to have discovered a source of unlimited free power were pure
fantasy, but it is equally possible that this extraordinary mind had leapt into a realm of understanding that
is far beyond what anyone has achieved since. Who
knows what the world would be like today if Tesla had
had his way?

Although certainly the most fascinating practitioner
of hidden or forgotten science, Tesla was certainly not
the first or the last of his breed. Right up to the present
day underfunded scientists are working away on ideas
that just might change the world, but they are considered eccentrics at best and frauds at worst. The
American physicist, Philo T. Farnsworth, was another
such genius. Known and respected as a highly talented
inventor who had single-handedly solved most of the
engineering problems of the modern television,
Farnsworth later turned his mind to the problem of
nuclear fusion. His own notes indicate that, in a series
of experiments between 1959 and his death in 1971, he
solved problems that researchers are still battling with
today.

The dream of nuclear fusion was the holy grail of the
post-war years. The power of the atom had already
been amply demonstrated by the atomic bombs used
on Japan in 1945, but they were examples of nuclear
fission. In a fission reaction large amounts of energy
are produced by effectively destroying atoms of heavy,
radioactive elements such as uranium. A fusion
reaction creates far greater energies by forcing atoms
of light elements, such as hydrogen, to fuse together.

This is the process that fuels the sun. It is sought after because it allows huge amounts of energy to be produced, it creates no dangerous nuclear waste, and the fuel can be derived from sea water. Unfortunately, to date, nobody has managed to create a fusion reaction that didn't require more energy to get it started than the reaction itself produced – unless Philo Farnsworth's claims are to be believed.

Most modern fusion experiments use apparatus the size of a small building and rely on extremely powerful electromagnets to contain the incredibly hot plasma in which the reaction is supposed to take place. The reaction chamber of Farnsworth's apparatus was about the size of a softball and sat comfortably on his desktop without the need for any kind of containment field. The first reactor, which Farnsworth dubbed the "Fusor", was built in 1959, when the scientist was working on a phenomenon he had discovered during the development of high frequency tubes for use in televisions and other equipment. Farnsworth discovered that a certain kind of tube could produce a tiny, incredibly bright point of light – actually a form of plasma – suspended in mid-air. He named these artificial stars "poissors". It was these poissors, self-focusing, energetic points in space, that provided the key to fusion. His results were spectacular: within a short time, and witnessed by dozens of other scientists, Farnsworth was apparently able to start and maintain a stable fusion reaction with a poissor, and then turn it off at will.

Once again the prospect of virtually free energy seemed a real possibility, and once again the hope was dashed. Funding for Farnsworth's research was suddenly and mysteriously cut. The patents for the

Fusor fell into the hands of the organization Farnsworth had been working for where they were promptly shelved as "unfeasible". Farnsworth himself, now in failing health, never recovered from the blow and died in 1971 without getting the opportunity to duplicate his experiments. Governments continued pouring billions into "big-machine" fusion research without result and the world carried on paying its electricity bills and gobbling up the planet's rapidly diminishing fossil-fuel reserves.

Perhaps the greatest dream of modern science is the ability to overcome the force of gravity. Unlike nuclear fusion, however, there appears to be no natural precedent for an anti-gravity field, and it is dismissed as totally contrary to the laws of physics by most scientists. Dr Eugene Podkletnov of Finland's Tampere University of Technology probably would have agreed with this assertion, until something very strange began happening in his laboratory. Podkletnov and his team were carrying out research into the behaviour of superconductors – materials that lose all electrical resistance at very low temperatures. They were using a device that consisted of three ceramic disks spinning at speeds of 5000 revolutions per minute, suspended in the magnetic field of three powerful electromagnets and enclosed in a liquid-nitrogen-cooled chamber. One day a colleague walked into the lab smoking a pipe and Podkletnov noticed that the smoke from the pipe was behaving very oddly when it passed over the top of the machine. Instead of spreading out randomly, as it was in the rest of the room, the smoke would suddenly rise straight up to the ceiling as if it were being pushed by some unseen force.

Intrigued, Podkletnov investigated further. The first

thing he noticed was that air pressure directly above the apparatus seemed to be slightly lower than elsewhere in the room. Hardly daring to address the thought that was forming in his mind, Podkletnov tried placing objects above the machine and weighing them. Incredibly, he found that these objects appeared to weigh up to two per cent less when they were above the superconductor experiment. It looked a lot like the device was shielding them slightly from the effect of gravity, a phenomenon that could also explain the drop in air pressure. Podkletnov persisted in his investigations, and he and the rest of the team racked their brains for an alternative explanation for what they were seeing. They even tried placing an identical apparatus on top of the first and discovered to their amazement that the effect was doubled – objects now weighed up to four per cent less when above the machines. Apparently they had stumbled on a form of anti-gravity. If the effect could be refined and strengthened the implications could be tremendous.

Like the good, conscientious scientist that he is, Podkletnov wrote up his results and submitted them to a respected scientific journal for publication. The *Journal of Physics,* a publication of the British Institute of Physics, could find no fault with Podkletnov's methods and agreed to publish his astonishing findings. Only then did the good doctor make an announcement to the press. The article which appeared in the *Sunday Telegraph* newspaper on 1 September 1996, was headed "'Anti-gravity' device gives science a lift". Not for the first time it looked like the world was on the brink of a scientific revolution. Many people had claimed to have built anti-gravity devices before, but none of the stature of Dr

Podkletnov. The fact that he was only claiming to have discovered a small, but significant, effect rather than a full blown anti-gravity machine also lent weight to his claims, as did the approval of the *Journal of Physics.*

Then, suddenly, only nine days after he had made the announcement Dr Podkletnov contacted the *Journal of Physics* and requested that the editor withdraw his paper from publication. Shortly afterwards a spokesman for the Tampere University denied that anti-gravity research was being carried out there, and a scientist credited with co-authoring the paper came forward to say that he had never heard of the project. It began to look like the whole thing had been a massive hoax, except that Podkletnov himself continued to insist that the phenomenon had been real. He refused to comment on why he had withdrawn the paper. There were rumours that certain nameless "funding agencies" had put pressure on Podkletnov not to reveal the details of his experiment and, since 1996, nothing more has been heard of the man or his anti-gravity effect.

There is a sense of incredible frustration created by all three of these cases. Machines or techniques that could have revolutionized the way we live have been dangled before our eyes and then snatched away, never to emerge again. It is very tempting to believe the conspiracy theorists who say that inventions like Tesla's free energy network or Farnsworth's desktop fusion reactor have simply been suppressed by super-government forces who are protecting their power by maintaining the status quo. It's an often quoted fact that three-quarters of the world energy is consumed by one-quarter of its population – the industrialized West – and it is certain that the sudden availability of almost free power would create a worldwide revolution with highly unpredictable results. But would governments really withhold such information, and could they do it even if they wanted to?

An argument against the conspiracy theory points out that the patents for many of the devices mentioned here are available for inspection by anyone. Blueprints for many of Tesla's devices at least are freely available on the Internet – if anybody really wanted to construct his free energy apparatus there is nothing stopping them apart from a little capital and same basic electrical engineering knowledge.

The advocates of the conspiracy theory come back with the argument that the cover-up is far more subtle than that. We are all so used to a world in which electrical power has to be bought that we cannot imagine an alternative, even though it's a state of affairs that has existed in most places for little more than a century. We are used to a world in which mysterious men and women in white coats carry out experiments that are far too complicated for ordinary mortals like us to understand, a world in which hidden and unaccountable funding organizations decide what is investigated and what is released on to the market for our passive consumption. Maybe all these scientists were mad, bad or mistaken; or maybe they were just as smart as they appeared to be and their discoveries have been taken from us by sinister forces protecting their own interests.

No Brainer

•••••••••••••••••••••••••••••••••••••

It's all in your head – or is it?

Of all the mysteries and miracles of the human body the function of the human brain is the most wondrous and the most poorly understood. Decades of research into the workings of the brain have allowed scientists to identify certain areas that they believe are connected with certain abilities such as speech, vision or motor skills, but the real mystery is how the brain works as a whole to create our overall consciousness. It is taken for granted by most people today that our minds and our brains are essentially the same thing. Popular science promises us a time when the electrical activity in our heads can be downloaded on to a computer storage medium, and then rebooted in an artificial body that will enable us to live for ever. Those people who invest in a cryogenic funeral, where the body is kept at extreme sub-zero temperatures in the hope that it can one day be revived, often opt for the cheaper alternative of having only their heads frozen – the sacred receptacle of the brain.

Philosophers concerned with the relationship between the mind and the brain often envisage "thought experiments" in which a living brain is suspended in a tank of nutrients and hooked up to a super-computer that recreates the electrical inputs that we usually receive from our senses. The question is, would you be able to tell the difference? Science fiction writers have leapt on the idea and spun tales in which people who are nothing more than brains in vats believe themselves to be walking, talking individuals in a real world. The hit 1999 movie *The Matrix* is just the latest in a long line of such stories. Our attempts to understand the brain are at the heart of our attempts to understand the universe and our relationship to it. Over the centuries views have changed radically. Before the advent of modern medicine the brain was not regarded as particularly important, the heart was generally considered to be the seat of personality and "soul". Later, the brain was seen as an extremely complex and subtle biological machine. Today, the most common analogy is with a super-computer.

The main difficulty with the popular modern view of the brain is that it fails to take into account the incredible resilience of this apparently delicate organ. The smallest damage to a complex computer almost inevitably results in the complete failure of the whole system. By contrast, even quite profound trauma can be shrugged off by the remarkable grey mass in our skulls, which seems to be able to re-route or relocate vital functions in a way that a fixed, circuit-based machine like a computer cannot hope to do. The story of Phineas P. Gage is a classic case in point.

In 1847 Gage was a construction foreman on one of the many railway building projects that flourished in the United States. One day, as he was preparing an explosive charge, a premature explosion drove a metre-long iron rod right through the centre of his skull. The rod entered his head just below his left cheek and emerged dead centre from the top of his cranium.

Incredibly he didn't even lose consciousness. Several hours later he was rational enough to ask if his accident had disrupted work on the line. For days afterwards Gage lay close to death, spitting out bits of skull and brain matter, but a few weeks later he was back on his feet and ready to go back to work. Gage had clearly lost a significant portion of his brain apparently without ill effect. Some reports say that his character was changed by the accident but whether that was due to brain damage or psychological trauma isn't clear.

Another astonishing case comes from the medical files of the state of California in 1981. Carpenter Michael Melnick thought his time had come when he fell ten feet through the floor of a house under construction. Amazed to find himself still breathing after the sickening crunch of the impact, Melnick tried to stand up, only to discover to his horror that a steel reinforcing rod embedded in concrete had been driven through his head and out between his eyes. The rod entered his head at the base of his neck, passed clean through his brain and emerged from the bridge of his nose. He was freed when workmates sawed through the metal rod and called an ambulance. Doctors were convinced that serious psychological problems would result from the brain damage but, after seven months, there appeared to be none. Melnick was left with insomnia and a fear of falling, as well as a great story to tell at parties.

It is an often quoted "fact" that we only use ten per cent of our brains. Since nobody knows exactly what is going on in any part of our brains at any particular time, it's difficult to see what this observation could be based on, but, in the light of cases like those of Melnick and Gage, there does seem to be an element of truth in it. When the brain suffers massive damage it seems to be able to move functions to other, unaffected parts. Whether this means that overall intelligence is spread more thinly or not is a very difficult question to answer. Even more extreme cases in which people seem to be born with almost no brain at all seem to suggest otherwise.

A programme on British television entitled "Is Your Brain Really Necessary?" addressed a mystery that has been puzzling scientists for years. Several people featured on the programme, identified only by false names, appeared to lead perfectly normal lives with almost no brain at all. A subject named Roger was shown to have no more than five per cent of the normal adult mass of brain matter. Amazingly, Roger has a first-class degree in mathematics and an IQ measured at 126. The whole area of his brain that scientists insist should control speech, emotion and the higher functions of conceptual thought are simply not there. Another perfectly normal member of society, identified as Sharon, was discovered to have a huge cavity where the frontal hemisphere of her brain should have been – again the areas associated with emotion and conscious thought. A young man named Stephen passed five "O" levels and functioned as a normal human being, despite the fact that the emptiness of his head could be dramatically demonstrated by holding a bright light behind it so that it glowed like a fluid-filled balloon.

A better documented case occurred in 1984 when Andrew Vandal was born in the United States. Doctors informed Andrew's mother that a cyst had formed on the stem of his brain when he was a foetus and that this had prevented the rest of the brain from developing. It was a recognized but very rare condition known as hydrancephaly which leaves the brain cavity filled with nothing but fluid. Despite the doctor's worst predictions Andrew was very much alive and kicking when he celebrated his fifth birthday in 1989.

Andrew has effectively no brain at all apart from the very basic brain-stem that we share with virtually all vertebrate animals, which allows him to breathe and perform simple movements. Despite this he is described as a happy child with an outgoing personality who constantly laughs and smiles. He cannot speak and, although his eyes are undamaged, he is blind. Scientists have suggested that the movements and characteristics that his mother and friends interpret as humour and personality are nothing more than reflex actions, or very simple learned responses, and that Andrew cannot possibly be thinking in the sense that we understand it. His mother, not surprisingly, disagrees. She also has two other, adopted, children with the same condition which would seem to suggest that her expertise is considerably greater than that of the doctors.

Extraordinary cases like these are not new. For years autopsies have been turning up near-empty skulls that belonged to apparently normal, healthy human beings. Most of these cases have been simply ignored by a scientific establishment unwilling to question basic concepts about the relationship between the mind and the brain, but these are exactly the concepts that such cases force us to consider. If a person can live a normal life with only a fraction of a brain, then the brain cannot be the defining factor of intelligence and personality. But if we only need a fraction of our brains to operate, what is the rest of it for?

Researchers into psychic phenoma often suggest that the apparently unused portions of the brain are the seat of mental powers that lie dormant in most of us. Powers such as telepathy, telekinesis or premonition certainly seem to exist in some individuals. Perhaps these people have found a way to unlock the unused potential of the human brain. An investigation into the psychic potential of people in whom large parts of the brain are absent might yield some answers. Until then, or until we gain a better understanding of how the brain functions as a whole, the true nature of the mysterious organ inside our heads will remain the most tantalizing of all questions. After all, it's worth remembering that the very thing we are thinking about when we consider these questions is the thing that is doing the thinking. It's the ultimate paradox and symbol of the human condition – an entity that does not know its own nature.

Two of a Mind

●●●●●●●●●●●●●●●●●●●●●●●●●●●●●●●●●●●●

That's just what I was thinking

There are few things more startling to the human mind than coming across identical twins. We are so used to the individuality of the people we meet that to find two human beings who look, act and sound exactly alike is more than a little disturbing. It's very hard for those of us who are not twins to imagine what it is like for there to be somebody else so similar to you that other people cannot tell you apart – we are obsessed by the idea of our own uniqueness. In a number of cases the likeness of twins has been shown to be far more than skin deep. Examples of identical twins with the same tastes, ailments and life stories are familiar and common-place. In a few cases these similarities are so extreme that it's difficult not to conclude that there is something far more than genetics going on.

In 1979 Jim Lewis met Jim Springer. The two men were identical twins separated at birth and meeting for the first time at the age of thirty-nine. It quickly became apparent to both men that either their lives were connected on a deep, mysterious level, or they had been subject to an unbelievable sequence of coincidences. Both men were compulsive nail biters, both had suffered from extreme migraines for a short period in their lives (the same period), both had heart problems and were exactly the same weight. So far the similarities are remarkable but nothing that couldn't be explained by their having an identical genetic make-up. Comparing their life stories, however, the coincidences began to get too weird.

Both men had married women called Linda, got divorced and then married women called Betty. Both had had the same jobs at some point. Both had sons, whom they had both named James Allen, smoked the same kind of cigarette, had dogs named Troy, spent their holidays at the same beach resort; and so the list goes on. It was almost as if two men, who looked identical, were living identical lives in different parts of the United States. The remarkable synchronicity of lives like those of the Jim twins has been seen as powerful evidence for a kind of human programming or predestination. It almost seems as if these two men, who knew nothing of each other, were compelled to live the same life. Whether this compulsion was genetic in origin or lay at a level still hidden to us we are powerless to say.

For centuries philosophers and theologians have waged war over the issues of free will and predestination. The arguments for predestination are difficult to refute and have cropped up time and again throughout the history of thought. As powerful as these arguments are, they are strongly opposed by the intuition that we are in control of our own actions and lives. Fatalists have argued that we are just material beings living in a material universe, and that every action in such a universe must have a particular and fixed reaction determined by laws of nature. It's only because the world is so complicated, involving billions of events acting on, and reacting to, each other that it looks like the future is uncertain. If we had a powerful enough computer, say the fatalists, programmed with all the physical rules of the universe and the current state of everything in it, we could say exactly what was going to happen at any point in the future.

Belief in predestination is not restricted to material-ists, there is a long tradition of theological predestina-tion. The Pilgrim Fathers, who settled the North American continent, for example, believed that the fate of every individual soul is decided by God before it is born. For the Pilgrims nothing they could do in their lives would make the slightest difference to the ultimate fate of their souls. Many Eastern religions have strong elements of predestination, relegating the individual to a helpless cog in vast cycles of creation and destruction that roll on over millennia, totally beyond our control.

The case of the Jim twins and others like them have been used as proof of the inevitability of the course of our lives. The argument goes like this: our genetic make-up and the circumstances of our birth deter-mine a very large part of what will happen to us and what we will do in our lives. The Jim twins had an identical genetic make-up and the circumstances of their births were very nearly identical. The lives that each of the Jim twins experienced, without any direct influence on each other, turned out to be far more similar than can be accounted for by pure coincidence; therefore everybody's life must be predetermined at birth. Many people find this kind of argument very hard to accept because it means that when we think we are making choices, for example when Jim Lewis decided to name his son James Allen, we are just doing what has already been pre-ordained.

Those opposed to the predestination argument often try to explain the coincidental lives of identical twins as the result of some form of telepathic connection. Another well-known phenomenon connected with identical twins is instances of empathic connection – where one twin feels what the other is feeling although separated by great distances. In July 1948 Alice Lamb was terrified when she was thrown off her chair by a huge, unseen force that struck her left side. Lying breathless on the floor, she felt a searing pain in her chest, later shown to be the result of two fractured ribs, and a sense of enormous shock. At the precise moment Alice was experiencing this phantom blow, her identical twin sister, Dianne, was being thrown violently from her train seat as the carriage she was in was derailed. Dianne broke two ribs in the accident. She was more than a hundred kilometres away when the trauma of her train wreck somehow leapt spontaneously to her sister.

Today science has a pretty convincing explanation for the existence of identical twins, if not for the extraordinary coincidences that seem to characterize their lives. The biological term for identical twins is monozygotic twins – meaning two individuals formed from one egg. Non-identical twins are known as dizygotic. In ancient times twins were regarded as strange and supernatural. For one thing far fewer twins, identical or otherwise, would have survived into adulthood in times when infant mortality was far higher than it is today, so their rarity value would have been considerably greater. Secondly, most cultures that believe in an all-powerful creator God, like Christian Europe, regard each individual as the creation of God. If that God sees fit to create two identical individuals, he must have some special purpose in mind.

The strangeness of identical twins is carried over into some of the most haunting supernatural phenomena. The doppelgänger or fetch is a persistent and powerful image in ancient and modern folklore. Doppelgänger is a German word that translates as "of himself". It is a common belief that everyone has a doppelgänger or double of himself somewhere in the world. Some people take this to mean that there is simply another person that looks just like you, while others imply a more uncanny origin for the double.

A celebrated case featuring a mysterious doppelgänger is that of Emélie Sagée, a French school teacher whose double was seen by dozens of people, although never by Emélie herself. Soon after starting work at a girls' school, her pupils were astounded to see an exact double of their teacher standing behind her and mimicking her actions as she wrote on the blackboard. Thirteen of the girls who had seen the double testified that although it was identical in appearance and manner to Ms Sagée, it did not have a piece of chalk in its hand as she did. On another occasion the double was seen standing behind Emélie as she ate dinner in the dining hall. Once again although it was exactly mimicking her actions, it did not hold a knife and fork. Ms Sagée's doppelgänger was usually seen very close to her, but she would only become aware of its presence when she heard the gasps and screams of other witnesses. When questioned about these events Emélie reported that she remembered feeling weak and emotionally drained, a sensation that subsided when the apparition vanished. Eventually Ms Sagée was dismissed from the school because of the disruption her uncontrollable apparition caused. On hearing the news she sighed and owned up that the same thing had already cost her more than a dozen jobs.

In this, as in almost all cases of the supernatural, the evidence is compelling and yet slim and untestable. All we have is the word of the witnesses and of Ms Sagée herself. A remarkable parallel with the imitating doppelgänger story, however, turned up in circumstances beyond doubt in a 1980 court case in York. The Chaplin twins, Freda and Greta, were on trial for assaulting and harassing a Mr Iveson, their next-door neighbour. The case was interesting in itself, a kind of psychological fixation had gripped both women where the unfortunate Mr Iveson was concerned. Both had an erotic obsession with him that manifested itself in constant abuse, both physical and verbal. After fifteen years the victim of their obsession had had enough and decided to ask the courts for protection. What really attracted media attention was the Chaplin twins themselves. Their degree of similarity was incredible on every level.

At thirty-seven they were as physically similar as the day they had been born. The overwhelming impression was of a mirror image duplication. Not only their physical appearance but their behaviour mirrored exactly. When sitting side by side, wearing identical clothes as they had done since childhood, their actions would mirror exactly; if one raised her left hand the other would raise her right, not in response but at exactly the same time as if one brain were controlling both bodies. Any attempt to introduce differences were fiercely resisted by the twins. If one broke a shoelace, the other would simply remove the opposite shoelace. Given two identical grey coats with slightly different buttons the twins removed half the buttons from each and gave them to each other. Given two bars of soap they simply cut both bars in half and took one half of each. When interviewed, they both said that they believed they shared a mind and that they knew exactly what the other one was thinking or doing at any time. Their simultaneous behaviour has been seen as evidence that they possessed a kind of telepathy with each other that was permanently "on-line". If true, this is not far from saying that they "shared a mind".

Another set of twins with similar "mirroring" behaviour seem to disprove the shared mind theory. Studied by the popular psychiatrist Oliver Sacks, Michael and John, known simply as the twins, have been in state institutions in the United States since the age of seven. Once again their degree of physical and behavioural similarity is eerie. Both are severely mentally disturbed and brain damaged – the damage is, of course, identical in both brains. They are both autistic and psychotic. They also share some of the extraordinary mental powers sometimes associated with the mentally retarded. A classic example is their ability to give the day of the week for any date or year they are given. Give them a date, 16 July 1426 for example, and they will tell you what day of the week it was with a hundred per cent accuracy. They are also able to repeat number sequences with perfect accuracy after only one hearing – they have been tested up to 300 digits without showing any signs of strain.

The superhuman ability that interested Sacks most, however, was their ability to visualize prime numbers. A prime number is a number that can be divided only by one and itself, the beginning of the sequence is well known to any schoolchild "1, 2, 3, 5, 7, 9, 11 . . ." During his study, Sacks came across the twins engaged in a game that was causing them great amusement: they were swapping six-figure prime numbers. Sacks only knew they were primes by checking them in a mathematical table. There is no known simple mathematical method of checking if a number is a prime, the only way to be sure is by laboriously dividing it by all numbers up to half its value. Fascinated, Sacks took part in the twins' next game, having noted down some eight-figure primes from his book. At first astonished by this new player the twins quickly got up to speed and were soon plucking eight- and then ten-figure prime numbers from the air, apparently without the slightest effort. Soon they were on to twelve- and then twenty-figure numbers. Sacks had no way of checking if these were primes too since his tables only went up to ten figures, but he didn't doubt it for a second.

Nobody really knows how some people are able to perform these incredible mathematical operations. Tables of primes are compiled today by computers, which use their millions of operations a second to go through every possible calculation one by one. It seems very unlikely that the twins were simply doing the same thing but far faster than a "normal" brain could, or that they knew some mathematical law that allowed them to check every number. Sacks, and others who have studied these phenomena, believe that these individuals are able mentally to "see" the patterns of these huge numbers in the same way that you or I can visualize the numbers six or four as they appear on dice. We can recognize the pattern of these numbers without having to count the actual dots; perhaps the twins do the same thing with huge numbers – they simply recognize a number as having a

prime pattern, or not, without having to do the calculations to prove it.

In the context of the Chaplin sisters, who claimed to
share a mind, the case of "the twins" raises an interesting point. Both sets of twins display synchronized
mirror behaviour, which looks a lot like two bodies
under the control of one mind, but in the case of
Michael and John their prime game would have been
impossible if this were the case. The whole delight of
the game for them was to reveal new "prime pattern"
numbers to each other, something that would have
been rather pointless if it were the same mind coming
up with all the numbers. Psychologists have suggested
that what is happening in cases like these is an
abnormal balance of right and left brain functions.

Anatomists have known for some time that the brain
consists of two mirror image hemispheres connected
by a bundle of nerves known as the corpus callosum,
but the implications of this dual control have taken
longer to dawn on scientists. Studies of electrical
activity in the brain during various activities or experiences have shown that the left brain is primarily
concerned with logic and spatial activities. The right
brain is more active during dreaming and similarly
illogical, emotional activities. When listening to a piece
of music, for example, it is the right brain that hears the
piece as a whole and responds to the mood. The left
brain may kick in occasionally to pick out the sequence
of notes played by a certain instrument. In our daily
lives most of us are dominated by our left brains; it is
here that our sense of ourselves as individuals moving
forward through time is based.

In the case of "the twins" the left brain functions are
severely restricted, allowing the right brain to take

priority. It is the right brain that allows them to recognize such complex number patterns without the left brain interfering and asking for logical proof. Michael and John's quiet left brains are a result of physical damage. In the case of the Chaplin sisters the phenomenon is more likely down to conditioning. Having been together all their lives and never encouraged to develop individual personalities, the sisters' left brains did not develop into the dominant partners. Their obsession with symmetrical pattern and behaviour suggests that their sense of self has been taken over by the right brain which doesn't trouble itself with the logical difficulties of one mind in two bodies.

The Saint and the Devil

Strange bedfellows

On the 17 July 1429 Charles VII was crowned King of France at the ancient cathedral of Reims, as all French kings had been before him. The coronation was the culmination of one of the most extraordinary military campaigns in history. This was the Hundred Years War – decades of bloody conflict between the English and the French for control of the French crown. Until the day before the coronation the city of Reims had been in the hands of the enemy. Many people, including the new king, believed that their recent startling military successes were due to divine intervention working through the young girl known as Joan of Arc. Joan was near the throne as Charles was anointed with the holy oil that symbolized his divine right to rule. Also near the throne was Gilles de Rais – at twenty-five years old he was the youngest of the king's military commanders, and the man who had been charged with escorting Joan on her military campaigns. These two young people had developed a close relationship based on mutual respect. Within a few years both would be dead. Despite their closeness in life one would be remembered as a saint and the other as a devil.

Joan of Arc arrived at the court of Charles VII – then known as the Dauphin – in February 1429. She was a simple shephard girl from Domrémy in Lorraine, who told the incredulous and motley collection of soldiers and adventurers who made up Charles's camp that she had received messages from the Archangel Michael. He had revealed to her that Charles was the true king of France and that he would liberate the city of Orleans and be crowned in Reims. Her appearance galvanized the hesistant and badly organized retinue. With her absolute conviction in the truth of her vision Joan infected Charles with a sense of purpose that was to change the course of history. Almost immediately, with Joan riding in the vanguard, the Dauphin's forces began to make advances. Gilles de Rais, appointed Joan's protector by the Dauphin, rode by her side through a series of hard and bloody battles. Within six months Orleans was liberated and Charles was crowned. Everything was exactly as Joan had said it would be. Joan's visions told her that the king's success would continue, that Paris too would be liberated and the English driven from French soil. They also told her that these events would result in her imprisonment and martyrdom. Once again her vision didn't let her down.

The assault on Paris failed and Joan herself was taken prisoner at Compiègne by Burgundians allied to the English. She was taken to Paris to stand trial for heresy and witchcraft. She faced sixty-four judges who regarded her not only as a traitor, but as a dangerous enchantress clearly possessed by demonic forces. It's difficult to realize today just how remarkable a person Joan must have been. This was one of the hardest, most violent and superstitious ages in Europe's history. War, disease, famine and random violence were commonplace. It was an age of ruthless nobles who, unhindered by concepts of law or human rights, ruled over their subjects without compunction. The aim of most was just to survive, the more powerful were bent on gaining wealth and influence. This was not an age in which women could thrive. Dominated by male violence, these were times in which the few women who managed to make a mark could only do so by being even more ruthless than their male counterparts or by taking the dangerous path of religious purity. Dangerous because it was literally impossible for a flesh and blood woman to live up to the expectations of sainthood, and because to fail was to invite the most terrible condemnation.

The ideal of femininity in this period was dominated by notions of religious and moral purity. The virtues of virginity, chastity and devotion were seen as reaching their highest incarnation in the perfect woman. Joan met all these criteria effortlessly, and it was in this that her power lay. For Gilles de Rais, a typical example of his age, Joan was fascinating. Gilles de Rais was a nobleman from the Anjou region. He had been orphaned at an early age and raised by his grandfather, a man who had instilled the ruthless values of personal enrichment and total disregard for the lower classes in his grandson. Both men lived lives of debauchery and what would be regarded as staggering lawlessness by today's standards. He had joined Charles's retinue simply because he thought it would be the winning side. Then Joan arrived. Her utter conviction, openness and purity of character hypnotized the brutal, uncouth soldiers and commanders of Charles's army. She was examined by the ladies of the court, by clerics and theologians. Then the King simply handed command of his army over to this seventeen-year-old girl.

For the first time in his life Gilles de Rais found himself a part of a truly noble and moral crusade. That's not to say that Charles's campaign and his claim to the throne was any more "right" or moral than those of any of the other parties involved in the war, but Joan's motives were above reproach. She truly believed that her visions were real commands from her God and the inspiration this gave to the Dauphin's soldiers proved decisive. Her convictions and character were no less awe-inspiring for the sixty-four judges who sat to decide her fate. Unfortunately, they took the view that her powers originated from diabolical rather than divine influence. For the medieval theologian the question was not whether people could receive visions and supernatural instructions, the question was rather where these voices originated. In an age of death and destruction the reality of the devil was unquestionable – his works seemed to be evident on every hand. To the medieval mind Satan was the great deceiver whose favourite trick was to convince the weak to carry out his will by disguising himself as an angel or saint. For the opponents of Charles this was clearly what had happened to Joan. She was caught in the classic trap. The danger was always present for the woman who claimed to be the mouthpiece of God – that the same characteristics of resolution and visionary conviction could be interpreted as divine or diabolical.

Joan remained loyal to her vision to the end. She answered all questions honestly and openly and always refused to accept that she had been misled by the devil. Death was the only possible outcome. On 30 May 1431 Joan, now eighteen years old, was executed in the old market square in the city of Rouen. On her close-cropped head was a paper cap, the mark of the heretic. Around her neck was a notice detailing the sixteen counts on which she had been convicted, including

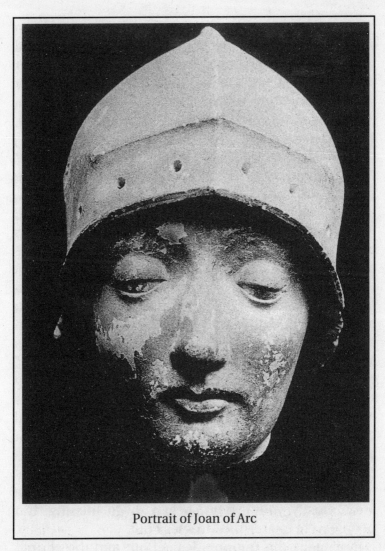

Portrait of Joan of Arc

falsehood, deception, devil worship and sacrilege. The fire that was to consume her was lit and the executioner had to withdraw before he could deliver the mercy of strangling the victim. According to tradition only Joan's heart was not destroyed on the pyre.

As if in despair at the glimpse of purity that had been snatched away from him, de Rais plunged into the kind of terror and debauchery that were to brand him for ever as a devil. De Rais's grandfather died soon after Joan's execution, leaving the family fortune in his hands. He embarked on a life of luxurious excess, staging sumptuous banquets and extravagant festivals that soon began to tell heavily on his estate. He also built churches and lavished money on their decoration to the point of absurdity. Eventually the king was forced to act, and he placed de Rais under a kind of house arrest, forcing him to sell off his estates piece by piece until his debts were paid. De Rais became involved with some dangerous and manipulative people, particularly a young cleric from Italy named Prelate, who convinced him that he could conjure devils and command them to make gold. De Rais had already been dabbling in alchemy in the hope of easing his financial problems and the sinister and satanic aspects of Prelate's "arts" excited his already disturbed mind. Dark and disturbing rituals were held in the castle and de Rais became convinced that he could see Prelate's devils. Local people began to fear their master even more now that brutality was accompanied by evil magic. Whispered rumours began to circulate that de Rais's occult rituals had moved into ever darker realms. Children from the area, mostly young boys, began to go missing, but people were too terrified to speak out.

Eventually the rumours leaked out and the church launched a secret investigation. Gilles de Rais was arrested and questioned before a tribunal of the inquisition. He treated the inquisitors with contempt and refused to give an account of his actions, an attitude that caused him to be excommunicated without hesitation.

Perhaps sharply reminded of how far he had fallen since the days he rode with Joan, de Rais broke down and made a full confession. Over an eight-year period he had murdered at least 150 children. Boys between the ages of about eight and fifteen were lured to the castle with offers of work. There they were kept captive, sexually assaulted and eventually brutally murdered by decapitation, slow bleeding or beating. The bodies were subsequently carved up and burned or disposed of in the moat. These crimes were not carried out by de Rais alone, a number of his associates were clearly involved in the abuse and murders, probably as part of the group's growing obsession with the occult.

The terrible catalogue of crimes could carry only one sentence; the double shame of hanging for murder and burning for heresy. Gilles de Rais and two of his man-servants were executed in October of 1440. On the scaffold de Rais asked for forgiveness from God and from the families of his victims. Before his lifeless body hanging from the noose was consumed by the flames, his heart was cut out at the request of friends at the royal court.

The Bleeding Blessed

Wounded heart

Images of Christ on the cross are familiar from churches all across Europe. Essentially they have remained unchanged for hundreds of years, but a closer look reveals something interesting about those created in the 500 years or so after the year 1100. This was the period that saw the first reformation in the Christian church. Ever since the church had became the official religion of the Roman Empire in the fourth century AD it had gradually been drawn into politics. By the turn of the first millennium the pope was one of the most powerful political forces in Europe and vied for influence with kings and emperors. A number of churchmen began to react against this increasing involvement in worldly affairs. These were the men who founded the orders of monks devoted to lives of abstinence and strict religious devotion. At the same time a greater emphasis was placed on the human face of Christ. Depictions of Christ on the cross that were produced under the influence of this new movement show him as very much a man, suffering real agony and shedding real blood. At about the same time a new and curious phenomenon made its first appearance. Known today as stigmatism, it was the sudden and spontaneous appearance of the five wounds of Christ on the bodies of ordinary men and women.

The first recorded case of the stigmata occurred on 14 September 1224. Francis of Assisi, future saint and one of the leading figures of the new church philosophy, was entering the second month of one of his many periods of religious contemplation. For a week he had been fasting and thinking about the suffering of Christ on the cross, then, one morning, as he knelt to pray, a strange transformation gripped his body. The event was described by witnesses:

> ... and his fervour grew so strong within him that he became wholly transformed into Jesus through love and compassion ... While he was thus inflamed, he saw an angel with six fiery wings descend from heaven. The angel drew near Saint Francis in swift flight, so that he could recognize him clearly as having the form of a man crucified ... After a long period of secret discussion this vision faded, leaving in his body a wonderful imprint of the Passion of Christ. For in the hands and feet of Saint Francis there began to appear the marks of the nails in the same manner as he had seen them in the body of Jesus crucified.

The wounds that Christ received during his execution were known to every Christian of the time from religious statues and paintings. He is shown with nails through the palms of both hands, a spike that penetrates both feet and a wound on his left side inflicted by a Roman centurion who stabbed him there with his spear. Some stigmatics have also exhibited a sixth wound to the forehead relating to the crown of thorns placed on Jesus's head. Francis of Assisi was already a known and venerated man of God but this exhibition of his closeness to Christ himself turned him into the most famous holy man of his age. As the story of the five wounds of Francis spread, so did the incidents of other stigmatics. Often they involved monks or nuns, although sometimes the "victims" were simple rural folk who became the wonder of a region and attracted huge crowds. Interestingly, it has been calculated that of all recorded cases of stigmatics almost eighty-five per cent have been women.

One of the most famous stigmatics of modern times was Padre Pio. Born in a small village in Italy, Pio entered a Capuchin monastery and soon began to exhibit the wounds that would make him famous. The first occurrence was on 20 September 1918, just three days after the brothers had celebrated the stigmata of St Francis. He was found unconscious on the chapel floor, where he had been praying alone, with blood pouring from the five wounds that had apparently spontaneously opened up on his hands, feet and abdomen. Although his bleeding slowed, it is said that the wounds never stopped flowing completely until the moment of his death in 1968. During that fifty years, Padre Pio never left the monastery, but tens of thousands of the faithful flocked there to receive his blessing. There is a strong movement in the Catholic church to have Pio canonized. Not only did he exhibit the stigmata but a number of other miraculous events were associated with him. He is claimed to have healed terrible afflictions on dozens of occasions, to have appeared at the beds of the dying despite never physically leaving his monastery cell, and to have told a young John Paul II that he would one day be pope.

As if the wounds of stigmatics weren't mysterious

enough in themselves, there is an established tradition of these wounds occurring according to a strict timetable. One Friday in April 1868 a young French girl named Louise Lateau displayed her stigmata for the first time. From that time on, for the rest of her life, they reappeared according to a strict schedule. Every Tuesday her stigmata points would begin to itch and tingle. By Thursday she felt shooting, stabbing pain and on Friday morning large blisters appeared which burst and gave way to flowing blood. By Saturday the blood and the blisters had disappeared, leaving only little pink patches on the skin which would remain normal until Tuesday came around again. Another clockwork stigmatic was Gemma Galgina whose wounds appeared every Thursday evening at eight o'clock sharp, bled all day Friday and were gone by Saturday morning.

Both Louise Lateau and another stigmatic, Therese Neuman, were extensively studied by doctors and other scientists. On one occasion researchers sealed Louise's arm in a glass tube on the evening before her wounds were due to appear, and were astonished to see the blood flowing on schedule without any possibility that she had inflicted the wound on herself. By the time she died in 1883 her stigmata had appeared 800 times. Therese Neuman's weekly experience began in 1918 when a vision cured her of blindness and other ailments that had made her bedridden by the age of twenty. Asked about what she saw during the period of religious ecstasy in which she bled from the hands, feet and eyes, she replied that she saw the whole scene of the crucifixion played out before her eyes.

Ever since the phenomenon first appeared in the

thirteenth century, the Roman Catholic church has claimed that the stigmata is a blessing bestowed by God to indicate those of special spiritual purity. Interestingly, in the period during which the Christian church has split into an ever-growing multitude of denominations, stigmata have appeared with ever increasing frequency in non-Catholics. In his book *World of Strange Powers*, Arthur C. Clarke records the case of Cloretta Robertson, a twelve-year-old school-girl from Oakland, California. During Easter week 1974, Cloretta was sitting in a maths class one morning when unmistakable stigmata suddenly appeared on her body – she even had the rare forehead wound of the crown of thorns. Cloretta's family belonged to the Baptist church, she and most of her classmates were black and from a culture a million miles away from the centuries-old traditions of Catholic Europe. Cloretta was exhaustively examined by doctors, some of whom saw the bleeding begin and noted that when the blood was wiped away there was no actual opening in the skin beneath. It was almost as if the blood were seeping through the skin itself. Cloretta continued her life as normally as possible; she was described by all who knew her as a cheerful and friendly character, even after it was discovered that she had developed healing powers as well.

Of the hundreds of reported cases of stigmata over the centuries, it is clear that a fair number must have been the result of self-inflicted wounds made by people desperate for adulation, or just those who simply wanted to emulate Christ's suffering on the cross. However, in cases like Cloretta's, there seems to be a genuine phenomenon that cannot be attributed to self-mutilation. Many theorists have suggested that stigmatic wounds are caused by the power of auto-suggestion – the capacity of the mind directly to affect the physical body, even to the point of causing bleeding without wounds. In almost every convincing case there was a powerful psychological cue that occurred just before the stigmata appeared. St Francis had been fasting and was in a heightened physical state highly receptive to visions. Padre Pio had just been through a festival celebrating the stigmata of St Francis and was no doubt contemplating that very thing in the chapel when his wounds first appeared. Even Cloretta Robertson was said to have watched a television documentary about the crucifixion which had given her strange and vivid dreams. Therese Neuman's weekly vision of the events on Calvary almost sound as if she were imagining the scene as hard as she could, in order to induce sympathetic wounds on her own body.

In recent years it has been pointed out by many historians that the traditional wounds suffered by stigmatics cannot be true imitations of the wounds of Christ because they are in the wrong places. Although Christ is traditionally shown on the cross with nails through the palms of his hands, it has been conclusively proved that the Romans did not crucify people like that. The hand is not a sturdy enough structure to support the weight of a dying body, nails would have simply ripped through the flesh and the victim would have fallen from his cross. It is far more likely that nails were fixed through the bones of the wrist. Not long after these conclusions became generally known, stigmatics with wounds in their wrists began to appear. Before then the stigmatics' only model had been the traditional depiction of the crucifixion seen in innumerable churches and religious texts. Another point that has been raised many times concerns the wound in Christ's side. The gospel of St John says only that a soldier stabbed Christ in the side, it does not say the left side, although this has been the established tradition for centuries. Stigmatics invariably have a wound on their left side.

Beyond the field of stigmatics, doctors have noted numerous cases of spontaneous bleeding or wounding that have nothing to do with religious experience. A Swedish physician documented the case of a woman who, at the age of twenty-three, had been badly beaten up and thereafter began to bleed from her eyes, nose and head every couple of weeks. Her physical wounds had long since healed and there were no signs of self-inflicted wounds at the bleeding sites – the skin was not even broken. An American doctor recorded over sixty cases of people in highly charged emotional states who could will their own bodies to produce weals, blisters, bruises and bleeding within the space of a couple of hours. During the later stages of World War II a veteran soldier blasted in a shell explosion became part of an experiment that clearly demonstrated the power of auto-suggestion. The blast had left him blind, although doctors could find nothing wrong with his eyes, and it was decided to try and use hypnotherapy to recover his sight. Over several sessions the soldier was taken back to the events of the day during which he was nearly obliterated by the artillery barrage. Occasionally his sight returned for brief periods, but other strange effects began to manifest themselves. On one occasion the soldier described being struck by a shell fragment in the hand. He had in fact received no such injury but the hand duly began to swell and started bleeding. Doctors found that they could induce minor wounds in their patient simply by suggesting them during hypnosis.

As incredible as it may be, there seems little doubt that extreme states of religious or other emotional stress can allow a person to inflict wounds on themselves simply by an effort of will. In the case of stigmatics they see the process backwards – a vision of the wounds of Christ that comes from somewhere else allows them to receive the same wounds. For those not inclined to believe in supernatural visions, the explanation works just as well the other way around – prolonged visualization of the wounds of Christ and his suffering cause the body to take on the same wounds in sympathy. Either way an interesting question remains. Many people suffer from extreme emotional stress and many people have a powerful devotion to Christianity, yet only a few of them develop stigmata-like wounds. What is it that sets these people apart? Are their visions just more vivid than anyone else's or do they possess mental powers that are undeveloped in the ordinary human mind; powers capable of affecting the physical world by thought alone?

Undead, or Just Not-Dead?

Suckered by a Vampire

Veil-like curtains move slightly in the breeze of a warm, moonlit night. Beneath the canopy of her elegant four-poster bed a beautiful young woman stirs in her sleep. The pure white sheets slip aside to expose the white, unblemished skin of her graceful neck, radiant in the moonlight. There is the slightest flutter at the open window and a figure, as black as the night, is standing over her. Cold, hypnotic eyes gaze down hungrily and the moonlight glistens on a cruelly hooked fang. There is a brief, strangulated scream and a single drop of ruby red blood . . .

The image of the vampire is so familiar that it can be conjured with a few words and the simplest of clichés. Far more than a mere monster to be hunted and slain, the vampire is one of the great anti-heroes of our era. Drenched in sexuality, power and the allure of immortality, the vampire legend has been interpreted again and again in books, comics and movies. Where did this potent figure come from? What in the experience of our predecessors invoked and fed this legend?

The origins of the vampire are buried too deeply in the human psyche to be unearthed. Ancient Greek and Egyptian tales make references to vampire-like creatures that were already firmly entrenched in folklore 3000 years ago. From Japan and Korea come stories of vampire women who could detach the upper half of their bodies and fly through the night in search of victims. Wherever these tales come from they embody three powerful ideas that have terrified and fascinated people since the beginning of time. Vampires live at night, the time when all respectable people are locked up at home; in an age of electric light at the touch of a button, we forget what terror the night held for our ancestors. Vampires drink blood, universally regarded as the essence of life; primitive cultures across the world have long believed that drinking the blood of your enemies allows you to steal their strength. Vampires are undead; the notion of a dead body reanimated by a dark and malign force has loomed large in the imagination of all cultures. The fact that a dead body looks uncannily like a sleeping body has always aroused the fear that the dead may wake.

The myriad branches of the vampire legend so familiar to the world today spring from Bram Stoker's fabulous novel of 1897, but the roots of that legend are embedded firmly in the centuries of plague and violence that preceded the Victorian age. In the fourteenth century the first great Bubonic plague crept across Europe. It was a time of terror quite inconceivable today. Nothing could stop the tide of death, nobody knew when or where the next outbreak would strike, and nobody was safe when it did. When this first pandemic eventually subsided nearly a quarter of the population of Europe was dead. In its place came a new and bizarre malady known as St Vitus's dance. In towns and cities across the continent a kind of mass hysteria broke out that drove people to dance insanely in the streets. Huge crowds of citizens, hysterical and foaming at the mouth, reeled and roared through the night streets like packs of devils. The fear and stress of imminent death from the plague had created a kind of madness of the collective mind. In this atmosphere of panic and paranoia about infection, reports of vampirism rocketed.

In a time when dead and decaying bodies blocked the streets, and few people could be found who were brave or foolhardy enough to dig graves for them, incidents of premature burial must have been horrifyingly common. In 1851 Dr Herbert Mayo of King's College, London, suggested that premature burials might go a long way toward explaining reports of vampires.

> *That the bodies which were found in the so called Vampyr state, instead of being in a new and mystical condition, were simply alive in the common way, or had been so for some time subsequent to their internment; that, in short, they were the bodies of persons who had been buried alive . . .*

It's not hard to see what Dr Mayo was suggesting. States of coma, trance or even unusually deep sleep have often been mistaken for death. An unfortunate individual recovering from such a state, only to find himself in a wooden box six foot under, is likely to attempt to scratch and dig his way out with every ounce of his strength before succumbing to lack of oxygen. If, for any reason, the coffin should be exhumed, the fingers and mouth of the victim would be found caked in his own blood and the body twisted and contorted. To superstitious witnesses in a time of plague paranoia the implication is clear – that the deceased has been rising from his grave and drinking the blood of others. If by some miracle the buried man was not yet dead and he still had the strength to reach out to his rescuers, his fate could well have turned out to be an unhappy one. Dr Mayo records the case of a man who was believed to have become a vampire.

> When they opened his grave . . . his face was found with a colour and his features made natural sorts of movements, as if the dead man smiled. He even opened his mouth as if he would inhale fresh air. They held the crucifix before him and called in a loud voice, "See, this is Jesus Christ who redeemed your soul from hell and died for you." After the sound had acted on his organs of hearing, and he had connected perhaps some ideas with it, tears began to flow from the dead man's eyes. Finally, when after a short prayer for his poor soul, they proceeded to hack off his head, the corpse uttered a shriek and turned and rolled just as if it had been alive . . .

As Dr Mayo suggested, this sounds chillingly like a man whose miraculous rescue from being buried alive was just the final twist in a fate too terrible to imagine.

The distinction between a corpse and a living, breathing person seems obvious but it has always been notoriously difficult to be sure. Heart-stopping stories of people who have been at the point of an autopsy knife before it was discovered they were still alive are still reported today, even in an age of heart monitors and brain scans. In days gone by, especially during times of disease epidemics, it must have been almost commonplace. In the early 1980s an eighteenth-century Parisian cemetery was dug up to make way for a car park. The specialists who relocated the coffins made the horrifying discovery that about a third of them showed signs that their occupants had tried to break out after burial.

Bram Stoker, author of *Dracula*, heard a near-premature burial story from his mother. Charlotte Stoker was a young girl in Ireland when a Europe-wide cholera epidemic reached her village in 1832. A local policeman, noted for his unusual height, was among the victims. When the undertaker tried to place his body in a coffin he found the man's exceptional loftiness presented a problem. Intending to break the man's legs, so that they could be folded over, the undertaker delivered a cracking blow with a large mallet he kept for the purpose. With a bellow of pain the supposed corpse leapt from the table and lived for many years to tell the tale.

Such tales of people "known" to be dead but later found to have moved in their coffins, to have bloody mouths and hands and torn funeral shrouds, fuelled the notion that the dead could rise and wander the night. The novelist Dennis Wheatley has also pointed out that graveyards were common refuges for vagabonds. Anyone catching sight of a ragged, gaunt figure slipping in or out of a burial ground late at night would be unlikely to enquire politely if he were a beggar or a member of the undead. These observations, coupled with the powerful psychological cues that the vampire legend plugs into – the waking of the dead, the power of the night, and the sanctity of blood – start to create a clearer picture of the origin of the modern vampire myth. For some people, however, the vampire is no myth.

In January 1973 a young police officer in the northern English town of Stoke-on-Trent was called in to investigate a death. At No.3 "The Villas" PC Pye encountered an extraordinary and disturbing scene. The body of Demetrious Myiciura lay on his bed. Salt had been scattered all over the body, the blankets and around the room. A bag of salt lay between the dead man's legs, and another by his head. A mixture of urine and salt was found in various containers around the room. Outside, on the window ledge, there was another bowl containing human excreta and garlic. The pathologists who performed the autopsy reported that the man had died by "choking on a pickled onion".

Pye was appalled and intrigued. A quick check at the local library confirmed his suspicions. The unfortunate Mr Myiciura, who was described as a Polish immigrant despite his very un-Polish name, had been trying to defend himself from vampires. Salt is a traditional vampire repellent and the obnoxious containers around the room and outside the window were traps designed to lure the vampire with their smell and then poison it. Pye shared his insights with the coroner who ordered that the fatal "pickled onion" be re-examined – it turned out to be a clove of garlic. The man had been sleeping with it in his mouth as an added deterrent to unwanted night-time guests. Whatever convinced Mr Myiciura that vampires were after him it was compelling enough to virtually dominate his life.

Another sensational case in London demonstrates the power of the vampire. In 1974 David Farrant, president of a group calling itself The British Occult

Female vampire

Society, was sentenced to five years in prison for the desecration of graves and outrages against public morality. Farrant had been one of many people who had become convinced that a vampire had taken up residence in London's famous Highgate Cemetery. The scare began five years earlier when a group of occultists had broken into a tomb and encountered an eight-foot-tall figure dressed in black who pursued them as they ran screaming from the site.

More strange encounters were reported until, on 13 March 1970, a mass vampire hunt was organized. More than a hundred people descended on the graveyard wielding crosses, stakes and garlands of garlic. Many claimed that they saw the Highgate

Vampire that night, a few even claimed to have tracked it to its lair and staked it through the heart. Whatever really happened, morning light revealed several thousand pounds worth of damage to graves and monuments, and the corpse of a woman who had been dragged from her grave. With something as powerful as the myth of the vampire, we can never be sure it is finally dead and buried.

Flying Nuns and Friars
• •

The only way to fly

Ever since the great English physicist Newton stopped a falling apple with his head, the law of gravity has been common knowledge. Newton formulated his insight like this: "Every body attracts every other body with a force that is directly proportional to the masses of the two bodies and inversely proportional to the square of the distance between them." He used it to explain why things are heavy, why everything falls downward and why the planets orbit the sun. It is generally agreed to be one of the most successful and unshakeable scientific theories of all time. Although few people could state the law in its full form, we all know what it means: "what goes up, must come down", and there are no exceptions. But if that is so, why is history littered with accounts of people to whom the law did not seem to apply at all?

In the late 1970s Padre Leone Haberstroch, one of the Roman Catholic church's most experienced and respected exorcists, told newspaper reporters that he would never perform another exorcism because he feared the devil would kill him next time. The terrors that had so frightened this stalwart man of faith were connected with the experiences of an Italian nun known only as Sister Rosa. The unfortunate sister had apparently spent almost a decade in the clutches of diabolical forces that had tried to mutilate, humiliate and kill her in a variety of bizarre ways. A string of exorcists had fled from the phenomena that assailed Sister Rosa, Padre Haberstroch being only the latest.

Priests and nuns told how they had witnessed Sister Rosa being beaten by an iron bar that had materialized in her cell as she slept. Kitchen knives had a habit of flying from tables as if to stab her, and ropes had uncoiled and wrapped around her neck to strangle her. In frequent attacks of demonic possession, Sister Rosa herself had assaulted other nuns and attacked the altar, screaming obscenities. Rosa could not even rely on the force of gravity not to turn against her – terrified sisters had seen her rise into the air, float towards the high ceiling and then pass right through it. She was found standing on the floor above in a state of shock. Levitation has always been associated with demonic powers in the Roman Catholic church, so it was this episode that shocked and horrified Rosa and the other sisters more than any other. The mother superior of the convent called in Padre Candido, said to be Rome's most senior exorcist, but the ultimate fate of Sister Rosa has never been revealed.

The sensational case of Sister Rosa is by no means the only time when a woman of God has suffered in this way. One of the most celebrated cases of levitation is that of the sixteenth-century Saint Teresa of Spain. Born in the town of Avila, Teresa's first contact with the world that was to become her vocation came at the age of sixteen when her father housed her with an order of Augustinian nuns. Teresa soon found her calling and became a Carmelite sister in 1535. Ill health prevented her from fully participating in the life she had chosen until 1562, when she founded her own convent in her home town of Avila. Her devotion and administrative skill saw the convent expand into sixteen houses over the next twenty years. It was during this period that Teresa began to suffer "attacks" as she called them. Apparently the saint would be periodically overtaken by raptures that caused not just her spirit but her physical body to soar into the air. Many of these events were witnessed and Teresa herself recorded them in her autobiography – original copies of which still survive. She often speaks of attempting to resist these flying episodes as if she were ashamed of them:

> . . . you feel and see yourself being carried away you know not whither. For though we feel how delicious it is, yet the weakness of our nature makes us afraid at first . . . so trying is it that I would often resist and exert all my strength, particularly at those times when the rapture was coming on me in public. I did so, too, very often when I was alone, because I was afraid of delusions . . . It was impossible to resist at all; my soul was carried away, and almost always my head with it – I had no power over it – and now and then the whole body as well, so that it was lifted up from the ground.

On one occasion Teresa was terribly embarrassed by being raised up in full view of several nuns as she approached the altar. She begged them never to tell what had happened. During a church service Teresa felt an "attack" coming on and threw herself to the ground to try and avoid floating. The strategy failed and her nuns had to gather around their leader to save her the embarrassment of being seen levitating above her seat. During an investigation into the life of the saint carried out thirteen years after her death, Vatican inquisitors heard the testimony of a Sister Anne of Segovia:

> *Coming upon Teresa one afternoon in the convent chapel I saw her raised about half a yard from the ground without her feet touching it. At this I was terrified, and she was trembling all over. I moved to where she was and put my hands under her feet. I wept over her feet for something like half an hour while the ecstasy lasted. When she sank down she turned her head to me and asked me who I was and whether I had been there all the time.*

Once again Teresa begged the witness to say nothing of what she had seen. Sister Anne only broke her silence when compelled to do so by higher authorities in the church, as did nine other witnesses, including the Bishop of Yepes, who had similar incredible tales to tell.

The phenomenon of holy levitation is by no means restricted to female members of holy orders as the extraordinary case of Joseph of Copertino demonstrates. Joseph had a bad start in life. Born Guiseppe Desa in southern Italy in 1603, the future, "flying friar", was regarded as a clumsy, incompetent simpleton in his home town. At the age of seventeen he joined the Capuchin order of monks, but was soon expelled because of his apparent idiocy.

Eventually Guiseppe, now Joseph, was accepted into the Franciscan order and was ordained as a priest in 1628. Quickly a whole host of miracles began to be associated with the ungainly, poorly educated friar. He was known for his extreme devotion to his vows, so much so that he went out of his way to make his life as uncomfortable and harsh as possible. He wore a hair shirt, which he never removed or washed, slept on bare boards and mixed herbal concoctions into his food which caused anyone else who tasted them to vomit violently. If some doubted his sanity, no one questioned his total religious devotion.

Friar Joseph was known to break into ecstatic shouts and chants during church services but on one occasion, during a service in the chapel of the monastery where he lived in Naples, Joseph uttered a tremendous shriek and flew across the chapel to the altar. In Rome he was said to have levitated as he knelt to kiss the feet of Pope Urban III. On another occasion Joseph was walking with a fellow priest, Antonio Chiarello, in the gardens of the monastery. It was a beautiful summer day and Chiarello remarked, "How lovely is the heaven which God has made". Joseph suddenly uttered a shriek of ecstasy and flew into the air, coming to rest in the branches of a tall olive tree where he remained in a position of prayer. His stunned companion noted that the branches did not bend under him "as if he had no more weight than a bird". After an hour Joseph returned to his senses and almost fell as he clutched at branches in terror at finding himself at such a height. Chiarello had to fetch a ladder to get the stranded friar down.

Joseph became famous, and infamous. He was banned from many churches because his religious ecstasies disturbed the other monks, and unnerved the priests, who were not used to such direct manifestations of the power of the Holy Spirit. Despite these censures the strange friar's flying career continued unhindered. In one spectacular example a witness describes how Joseph caused chaos in a monastery:

> . . . *detaching himself swiftly from the altar with a tremendous roar like thunder, he went, like lightning, spinning hither and thither about the chapel, and with such force that he made all the cells of the dormitory shake, so that the monks rushed out in fear, crying, "Earthquake! Earthquake!"*

Apparently Joseph did not share St Teresa's embarrassment at his giddying powers. Even as Joseph lay dying, now a man of over fifty, doctors witnessed him rise from his chair in a trance and stay there for many minutes despite their best efforts to pull him back to earth. How are we to account for these blatant transgressions of Newton's law? Mass hallucination? Given the scorn that Joseph's acrobatics earned him that seems unlikely. Trickery perhaps? Again, unlikely, considering the profound faith possessed by both people, and the fact that St Teresa at least wanted nobody to know about her "attacks". Comments made by those who have witnessed these phenomena nearly always refer to a state of ecstasy that overcomes the subject. It's as if the mind or soul, itself on a rush of soaring emotion, infuses the body and takes it along for the ride. Everybody has experienced moments of elation when you feel "lighter than air", perhaps in the case of a few people the feeling becomes reality.

Levitation of St Joseph of Copertino

The Hero Who Never Was

●●●●●●●●●●●●●●●●●●●●●●●●●●●●●●●●●

The strange career of Major Martin

For a soldier in the winter of 1942–43, death was never far away. But for one soldier, who perished somewhere on the battlefields of the world's most terrible war, death was not the end. Exactly who this man was, and where he died, remains a secret, but we do know that, whoever he was, he saved the lives of countless other Allied soldiers and brought the end of the war a giant step closer. How could a dead man achieve all this?

By the early spring of 1943 North Africa had finally been brought under Allied control. The epic battle, fought by Generals Montgomery and Rommel – two of the finest military commanders of the war, was seen as a turning point by the Allies. Up until then they had suffered nothing but defeat after defeat at the hands of Hitler's seemingly unstoppable war machine. Now, at last, they knew he could be beaten. The British Prime Minister, Winston Churchill, described the victory in one of his now legendary speeches: "This is not the end; this is not even the beginning of the end, but it is, perhaps, the end of the beginning."

The Germans had been driven out of North Africa, but the whole of mainland Europe was under Nazi control, and the vast territories of the Soviet Union looked set to fall at any time. The Allies had to gain control of the Mediterranean and that meant stepping from North

Africa into Italy. The closest and best place for an invasion was Sicily. Unfortunately this was just as obvious to the Germans as it was to the Allies. Churchill summed up the problem with his usual directness: "Anybody but a damn fool would know it's Sicily." If the Allied armies tried a landing in Sicily they would be met by the full force of Axis power and cut to pieces before they got off the beaches. The problem was, how to convince German high command that the Allied strike would come somewhere else. Then somebody had an idea, but they needed a dead soldier.

On 30 April 1943, a British submarine surfaced under cover of darkness just 1600 yards off the coast of neutral Spain. Working swiftly, the crew unstowed a coffin-like canister, removed the body of a man from inside and dumped it into the sea. Military papers in the British Royal Marine uniform that the corpse wore identified him as Major William Martin. Handcuffed to the body's wrist was a briefcase containing documents vital to the future of the Allied invasion of southern Europe. Why was the Royal Navy delivering such sensitive information into the hands of the Germans? Because it was fake, and the courier, Major Martin, had never existed. During World War II Spain was a neutral power, but the Allies knew that the Spanish government was sympathetic to the Nazis and would readily share any information they came across. In one of the most secret operations of the war, a highly select unit within British intelligence had constructed an elaborate hoax to mislead the Germans into thinking that Allied invasion forces would strike Sardinia and Greece, not Sicily.

The two men who masterminded the operation, code-named Mincemeat, were Lieutenant Commander Ewen Montagu and Flight Lieutenant Charles Cholmondeley, members of a top secret security committee charged with the almost impossible task of keeping Allied objectives hidden from the Germans and, where possible, of putting the enemy on the wrong track. As the submarine returned from its macabre delivery run, it was just the start of a long and anxious wait for Montagu and Cholmondeley. Would the body be discovered? Would the papers be delivered into the hands of German intelligence and, above all, would they believe them? They were taking a big gamble: if the plan worked thousands of Allied lives could be saved in an unopposed landing on Sicily, but if the Germans saw through the deception, they would be absolutely sure that Sicily was the real target and the landing forces could be annihilated.

On 3 May, London received word from the British Naval Attaché in Madrid that the body of a Major William Martin had been found by Spanish fishermen off the coast of the town of Huelva, apparently the victim of a plane crash into the ocean. The attaché knew nothing of operation Mincemeat and simply reported that the major had been given a military funeral after an autopsy and other legal formalities had been carried out by the Spanish authorities. Among a select group of men the news of the dead man's funeral, and more especially the medical examination, was cause for tentative celebration. If the body had been in the hands of the Spanish authorities it was more or less certain that the briefcase had been opened and its contents shared with the German spy network. The only question was: would the Germans swallow the bait. German intelligence was efficient, experienced and sure to be suspicious of such a prize being delivered into their hands.

Preparation of the hoax had been meticulous. Among the personal effects the Germans would have found on the major were London theatre ticket stubs, a letter about an overdrawn bank account, a picture of his fiancée, love letters, a party invitation and a letter from an uncle complaining about rationing. The hardest part of the scam had been constructing the fictional major's military persona; above all there had to be a reason for a relatively low-ranking officer to be carrying such sensitive documents (the dead soldier had to be low ranking because the Germans knew all the members of Allied high command and could easily have spotted a fake). Montagu's solution was to make Major Martin an expert on landing craft on the staff of Combined Operations Chief Lord Mountbatten. Martin's rank was adjusted from major to captain-acting-major and he was on his way to head a training camp in Algiers. Among the dead major's orders was a letter from Mountbatten to Andrew Cunningham, commander of the Mediterranean fleet, asking that Martin be sent back to London as soon as possible and that he might "bring some sardines with him" – a cunning reference to the fake invasion objective.

Everything rested on one key document – a letter from vice chief of the Imperial General Staff, Archibald Nye, to the commander in Tunisia, General Harold Alexander, providing up-to-the-minute information about the planned invasions of Sardinia and Greece. The orders indicated that Sicily would also come under attack, but only as a diversion from the main thrusts of operations Brimstone and Husky – the fake codenames for the invasions of Sardinia and Greece. Nye's letter states that there seems to be a good chance of making the Germans "think we will go for Sicily – it is an obvious target and one about which they must be nervous". Within a few weeks of Major Martin's "arrival" in Spain, his personal effects, including the vital briefcase, were returned to London by the Spanish government. A painstaking forensic examination showed that the orders had been opened and then resealed. Churchill recieved a terse comuniqué "Mincemeat swallowed whole".

One of the most difficult aspects of the ruse had been to make the body of Major Martin a convincing air-crash victim. There was no shortage of bodies, but it had to be the right body for the job and there wasn't time to wait for a genuine air-crash at sea. A pathologist was consulted to detail the signs he would look for in such a case. The recommendation was for a victim of pneumonia and exposure – the fluid-filled lungs would look like drowning, and damage to body tissues caused by cold would be consistent with long exposure to icy Atlantic waters. Before launching the body into the sea, the submarine crew had secured an inflatable life vest around its neck to make it look like the major had survived the crash and then died later of the cold. It has never been revealed where intelligence found the body they needed, all we know is that he was a young man who died of exposure. There has been no shortage of speculation about his identity over the years. Some have claimed that he was actually a German who had died in North Africa and this is certainly not inconceivable; the British authorities may have been reluctant to use the body of a man who had died fighting for his country – especially if they knew his identity and could have given him a proper burial. Others have claimed that the man was in fact British and that his body was later secretly reburied at the tomb of the unknown soldier as a mark of respect for the service he had done after death.

There are apparently no clues as to Major Martin's true identity – even the photograph on his fake identity papers is of somebody else. This particular detail had been a real problem for Montagu and had looked like scuppering the whole operation. There was no available photograph of the dead soldier – a fact that some have seen as evidence that the dead man was a German – and all attempts to photograph the body so that it looked alive were a dismal failure. Without a photograph for ID papers, Operation Mincemeat was dead in the water. Then, by an incredible stroke of luck, Montagu met an officer who bore a striking resemblance to the dead man. Without letting him into the secret, Montagu persuaded the man to pose for a photograph and everything was ready to go.

On 10 July Allied forces stormed Sicily. To everyone's relief they met only light resistance and quickly established a firm hold on the island. As intelligence reports of enemy positions came in it became obvious that Operation Mincemeat had been a resounding success. The Axis powers had concentrated on defending Sardinia and Greece, the Germans and Italians had split their forces into two concentrations 800 miles apart, giving the Allies an almost open door into Italy. After the war, documents emerged which revealed just how convinced the Germans had been. A memo from the German Navy's commander Admiral Dönitz states: "The genuineness of the captured documents is above suspicion." The admiral also records in his diary that there had been a major row between Hitler and Mussolini over the expected invasion of Italy: "The Führer (Hitler) does not agree with the Duce (Mussolini) that Sicily is the most likely invasion point. He believes that the discovered British orders confirm that the planned invasion will be launched mainly against Sardinia."

It's a con

••••••••••••••••••••••••••••••••••••

There's one born every minute

The legendary circus impresario, P. T. Barnum, once famously remarked that "There's one born every minute", meaning of course that new and invariably gullible customers were being being born all the time. Like many people before and since, Barnum had discovered that human curiosity and an almost pathological need to believe could be very lucrative character traits. There are essentially two kinds of con; the one that appeals to greed and the one that appeals to our sense of wonder. Men like Barnum capitalized mostly on the latter; those whose scams include the classic selling of the Eiffel Tower or the Brooklyn Bridge rely on the first – with just a dash of wonder thrown in.

A classic case of a "wonder" con took place in upstate New York in 1869. George Hull, a cigar maker from Binghampton, asked his brother-in-law, William Newell, to dig a well on his property in a town called Cardiff, exactly twenty feet behind an old barn. Newell confessed that he thought it an odd place to dig a well, but he hired two men for the purpose and set to work with picks and shovels. Three feet down they struck rock – rock that looked surprisingly like a giant human foot. Within an hour the astonished diggers had uncovered the form of a ten-foot-tall naked stone giant. With surprising presence of mind, Newell erected a tent over the site and charged fifty cents for a look.

Within weeks, news of the fossilized giant in New York was the talk of the city. Newell's farm was not an easy place to get to, but, nevertheless, people flocked from far and wide. Stagecoaches ran daily from Syracuse, the closest railway stop, to Cardiff and up to 500 hundred people a day made the trek. The giant, still in the pit where it had been uncovered, netted Newell and Hull $12,000 before they decided to move on to bigger things. Selling an interest in the fossil giant to a syndicate of local businessmen for a further $30,000, the wonder of New York was moved to a permanent display site in Syracuse. Visitor numbers went through the roof. The railroad even scheduled a ten-minute stop in the town so that people could rush across the road and take a peek before continuing their journeys.

The giant was, of course, a fake. It had been carved from a solid lump of gypsum under Hull's direction and later buried on Newell's farm with his brother-in-law's full knowledge. A full year later the "discovery" was made. The inspiration for the hoax had come from the Book of Genesis which states "there were giants in the earth in those days". Hull and Newell had taken care to place their relic in an area that was known as a source of ancient archaeological finds and it fooled cartloads of experts. Others, however, were not fooled and the scam was eventually uncovered. The men who had done the carving confessed and witnesses came forward who said they remembered seeing a mysterious crate being delivered to Newell's farm the year before.

Amazingly the Cardiff giant became even more popular after it was exposed as a fake. The sheer wonder of the idea was enough to draw in the crowds.

P. T. Barnum later offered to lease the giant for $80,000. When he was turned down he simply had his own model carved, and set it up in a hall a few doors away from the original. Barnum's "fake" fake drew even larger crowds. Sometimes it seems we just want to be fooled.

Another case of a wish-fulfilling hoax had the scientific community fooled for forty years. Between 1911 and 1915 fragments of bone were discovered in a gravel pit at Piltdown in England. A human jawbone found near Heidelberg in Germany, and other discoveries across Europe, had whetted scientists' appetites for the study of the very early history of humanity. Now it seemed that there was a new and important discovery in England. The pieces turned out to be a part of a jawbone and the back quarter of a cranium – apparently from the same individual. Using reconstructive techniques scientists built models of what they thought Piltdown Man must have looked like. It was a strange hybrid with a very modern-looking forehead and cranium but a distinctly ape-like jaw. The models fitted so well with the established notion of our cave-dwelling ancestors as half-human, half-brute that few people thought to question it. The image of Piltdown Man still informs the popular idea of cavemen today.

It wasn't until 1953 that Joseph Weiner proved conclusively that the Piltdown skull was a hoax. The discovery of human remains from roughly the same period near Peking had raised suspicions in 1926. Peking Man's skull was much more modern-looking than the ape-like Piltdown Man, but nobody could be sure that it wasn't just a regional variation. After years of careful study, however, Weiner managed to piece the fraud together. The skull was actually that of a modern human which had been dyed to make it look older, and the jawbone was from a orang-utan similarly treated. The only question that remained was, who did it and why?

The prime suspect has always been Charles Dawson, the man who made the initial discovery. Dawson, an amateur palaeontologist working with a fossil collector named Lewis Abbot, told friends that workmen had uncovered something odd at a local gravel pit and that he intended to investigate. The place was swarming with collectors within days, few of whom remembered that Dawson had been the one to start the rumour. When the fragments were uncovered, Dawson was virtually forgotten in the furore. The skull was not the only fake find at the site. A few years later an elephant tooth, that turned out to be an ape tooth painted with artist's pigment, and a fossilized elephant bone, that had signs of scoring with a steel knife, were also uncovered. Presumably these were also planted by Dawson.

We will never know exactly why Dawson carried out his fraud. He gained little from it and died in 1916, taking his reasons to the grave. Probably he just wanted to win the respect of his professional peers, or even just ensure that his name was connected with a great discovery. On the other hand, it's hard to believe that Dawson didn't realize that his fraud would one day be uncovered. Perhaps that was all he wanted. It will certainly be remembered as one of the most successful scientific frauds in history.

Other people carry out their deceits with their eye on rather clearer objectives – usually money. Some have become legends for their ability to extract cash from people with the most incredible stories. "Count" Victor Lustig was one such. Remembered today as the man who sold the Eiffel Tower, Lustig is venerated by conmen as the greatest of them all. Born in Czechoslovakia in 1890, Lustig began his career in Europe and emigrated from France to the United States in 1920, when a number of shady deals began to catch up with him. His scams had seen him safely through the war years and his travels across the continent had enabled him to become fluent in several languages. He was undoubtedly a man with rare gifts.

Lustig continued his scams on the far side of the Atlantic. One of his favourite and most successful cons was his patented money-making machine. Time and again Lustig was able to persuade businessmen to buy a machine he had developed, and which he claimed could print totally realistic banknotes on ordinary paper. As amazing as it may seem, dozens of people, many of them experienced businessmen, were taken in by the scam. Duped by a demonstration in which the machine churned out real bills, they readily parted with thousands of dollars to have one of their own. Naturally when they tried it later the machine produced nothing more valuable than blank paper.

One day in 1925 Lustig read a newspaper report about proposed repairs to Paris's most famous landmark, the Eiffel Tower. The report gave Lustig the inspiration for one of the greatest scams in history. Back in Paris he had some very official and important letter-headed paper made up and sent letters to six of France's leading scrap metal merchants, inviting them to a secret meeting at a plush hotel in the city. Once the men were assembled Lustig, posing as "Deputy Director General of the Ministry of Mail and

Telegraphs", informed them, in the strictest confidence, that repairs to the Eiffel Tower had proved to be too costly and that the monument was to be torn down and sold as scrap. He urged his audience to keep the intelligence secret as the government feared public reaction would be negative. Once the work began, he assured them, nobody would be able to do anything about it.

The scrap metal dealers were enthusiastic. The thousands of tons of iron that make up the tower clearly represented millions of dollars worth of scrap. As the meeting broke up Lustig took one of the men aside and assured him that his firm would almost certainly be given the contract since it was considered the most reputable, although the decision remained to be made. The businessman knew an opportunity when he heard one, and within hours he was back with $100,000 as an incentive to choose his firm. Satisfied with his haul, Lustig left the city that night. He was astonished when the next day he could find no mention of his crime in the papers. Deducing correctly that his victim had been too embarrassed to approach the police, and therefore had probably not told his competitors about the sting either, Lustig decided to try for a second bite of the cherry. Back in Paris he contacted another of the dealers who had been at the meeting, spun the same story and netted another $100,000 as a "bribe" for the contract. Lustig was back in America counting his money when the scandal eventually broke.

Selling the Brooklyn Bridge, an engineering marvel first opened in 1883, may not be as spectacular a stunt as selling the Eiffel Tower, but George C. Parker managed it on average twice a week. Born in 1861,

Parker was in his early twenties when the bridge was opened and began to attract sightseers. He quickly developed a technique for squeezing money from gullible out-of-towners. Putting on a sincere and somewhat simple-minded character, Parker would stroll up to a visitor gazing at the marvel and casually inform him that he was the owner of the marvellous structure. Once a conversation had been struck up, Parker would let his new friend into a little secret – that he intended to set up a toll on the bridge and charge a cent for everyone who passed. When the victim pointed out that he could surely get more than that Parker just laughed and dismissed the suggestion as ludicrous. Eventually the victim would become so exasperated that he would offer to buy the bridge himself and set up his own toll.

Over twenty years Parker sold the Brooklyn Bridge hundreds of times using this scam. Depending on the wealth of his victim, he would charge between fifty and fifty thousand dollars. Naturally he preferred the big catch and had a network of spies to inform him when a potential customer was in town, but he enjoyed the con so much that he would gladly do it for fifty dollars and an afternoon's entertainment. Not only was Parker incredibly convincing, he also had official-looking deeds drawn up to back his claims. On several occasions the police had to arrest Parker's victims when they tried to set up toll gates on the bridge. Eventually in 1928 Parker was convicted of involvement in another scam. It was his fourth conviction and as such landed him with a mandatory life sentence. He died in Sing Sing prison nine years later.